MW01107286

Happy Colors!

Cozy Baker

THROUGH THE KALEIDOSCOPE

By

Cozy Baker

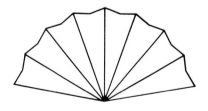

Beechcliff Books
Annapolis, Maryland

Printed in the United States of America
by Hagerstown Bookbinding and Printing

Library of Congress Catalog number 85-071412
ISBN: 0-9608930-1-6

Photo and Illustration Credits

No designs or photographs are to be utilized or
reproduced without the written permission of the artist.

On the covers: Images through Van Dyke, Ltd. Series II
photographed by Barbi Baker Richardson

All illustrations designed and executed by Jan Haber

Each floral abstraction and photograph taken though a
Karelitz Kaleidoscope or Karascope reproduced exclusively for this
book by Judith Karelitz copyright © 1985, N.Y.

All photographs taken through a Bennett Scopelens™ by
Carolyn Bennett copyright © 1985, Pa.

Photographs on pages 16, 49 (Bush), 50, 51, 52, 53 (interior), 57 top,
59 (3 on left), 60, 61 top, 63, 64, 80, 97, 101, 104 lower, 105 top,
107 top, 109 lower right.
photographed by Barbi Baker Richardson

Color photograph of Doug Johnson scopes photographed at New
Morning Gallery by Martin Fox, product stylist, John Cram

Laughing Coyote — black and white photograph by Mike Lennahan
color by Bill Tchakrides of Photography Associates

Classical Glass — photographer, Jack Bingham

Photograph of Carmen Colley by Brenda Day Ladd

Photograph of Mary Golden by Carol Dulac

Photographs of Pat Seaman, David Kalish, Tom Proctor
and Jeff and Tina Stasi, by Paul Seaman

Photograph of the author by Carolyn Bennett

All other photographs courtesy of individual artist.

Beechcliff Books
100 Severn Ave. Suite 605
Annapolis, Maryland 21403

This book is dedicated
to the designers, collectors
and lovers of kaleidoscopes

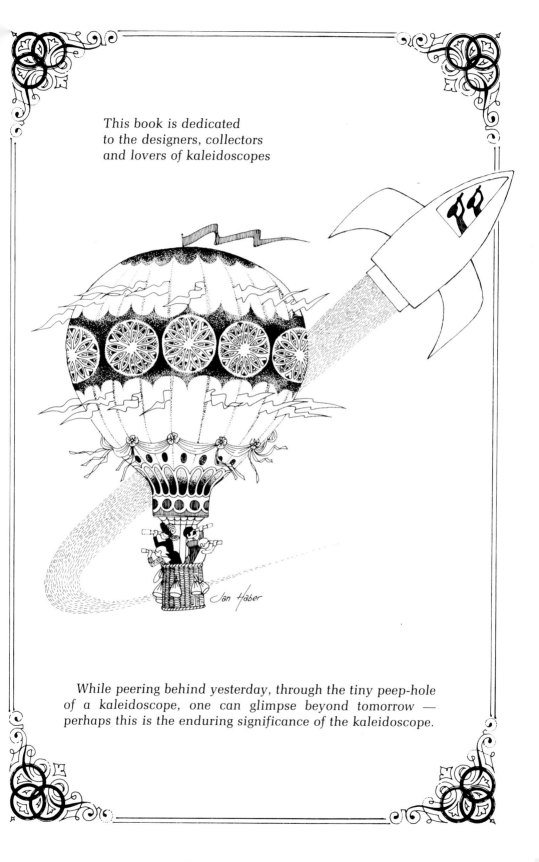

Jan Haber

While peering behind yesterday, through the tiny peep-hole
of a kaleidoscope, one can glimpse beyond tomorrow —
perhaps this is the enduring significance of the kaleidoscope.

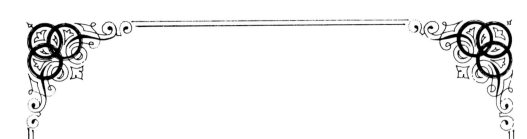

Special thanks and appreciation to

Barbi Baker Richardson, my daughter, for her stunning photographs on the front and back covers and others throughout the book,

Jan Haber for her many delightful illustrations,

Bea Moore for her editorial help,

Irene Walker for her thoughtful and sensitive input in all areas,

David Sale for his assistance in researching the life of Sir David Brewster,

Perk Hull, Art Director and Wayne Dixon, Account Executive at HBP for their caring helpfulness from beginning to end, and each person mentioned in this book for his or her complete cooperation and total support.

Table of Contents

Prologue		8
Foreword		9
Section I	Once Upon a Scope	11
Section II	New Images Emerge	19
Section III	Related Facets and Inner Reflections	95
Appendix I	Shops and Galleries Featuring Kaleidoscopes	130
Appendix II	Brewster Patent and Excerpts from Bush Patents	133
Bibliography		141
Index		142

Prologue

It was during my search for the other half of the rainbow that I found my first kaleidoscope. Rainbows have always intrigued me. As a little girl I was curious about the pot of gold at the rainbow's end. But even more, I pondered where the other half of the rainbow could be hidden. Surely a phenomenon so rare and beautiful must be a complete circle. Even at that early age, I must have been thinking in terms of mandalas.

Only in recent years have I come to understand why I could never find the other half of the rainbow; why, indeed, no one has ever come forth to announce the great discovery of that proverbial pot of gold. We have all been looking in the wrong direction. It isn't out there!

Just as the answers to life's secrets and mysteries are to be found within, so the hidden half of the rainbow exists in the individual heart. It is up to each of us to create our own inner rainbow, using shades and hues that reflect patience, tolerance, compassion and forgiveness. Every emotion is a color of life's rainbow. It is how we put the tones together that determines harmony or dissonance. While the rhythm of the visible rainbow seems to move from above, downward, the pattern of the eclipsed half flows from inside, out.

Concentrating on this concept, I searched the horizon of my mind for the most spectacular rainbow I could envisage. I had planned to assign a special pastel shade to each constructive thought and a vibrant jewel tone to every positive attitude, but a strange thing happened. The more I looked, the less color I saw.

Instead, I beheld light — glistening, gleaming, dazzling, radiant light. Brighter and brighter those arches grew; and then it dawned on me. The other half of the rainbow is light, which is the full spectrum of color. This glorious light illumines our hearts and minds; then, just like a kaleidoscope, it mirrors our thoughts and feelings to all our world.

And the pot of gold is love!

Foreword

During the past decade there has been a keen resurgence of interest in kaleidoscopes. Allowing the eye to marvel, the mind to explore and the soul to soar, these mirrored tubes of magic are being recognized and accepted as a valuable art form as well as an aesthetic and inspirational influence.

Since its invention by Sir David Brewster in 1816, the kaleidoscope has fulfilled a variety of functions. Universal in appeal, and spanning all age groups, it has served as a toy for children, a center of parlor entertainment for adults and as a design palette for artists, jewelers, architects, weavers, and rug and wallpaper designers.

The current renaissance embraces an interest and enthusiasm for the many evolving new styles as well as a respect for rare antique models. So join me in a look through the kaleidoscope — its origin, current developments, related facets and inner reflections.

Section I

Once Upon a Scope

Kaleidoscope
Its colors are the sparks from rainbows
Dancing, darting with endless surprise
Its patterns vibrate rhythmic motion
Unveiling magic before our eyes.

D Brewster

Once Upon a Scope

Images and colors have been reflected since water appeared on our planet, and objects have been multiplied since the advent of mirrors. But not until 1816 was this magic phenomenon put together in a visual capsule. Sir David Brewster took the first giant step in the creation of the kaleidoscope.

David Brewster was born in an obscure country town in the midst of the Scottish lowlands on December 11, 1781. He was somewhat of a child prodigy. While yet only ten years old, he constructed a telescope, significant of the chief bent of his work and genius. Nature endowed him with some of its choice gifts: close observation, unceasing inquiry, and a scientific proclivity. Far before his peers, he absorbed all that was available in elementary Scottish education. Because he evidenced exceptional aptitude for learning, his family decreed that he should study for the ministry of the Church of Scotland.

Thus at the tender age of 12, he was consigned to the University of Edinburgh where he continued his intellectual achievements. Indeed, he was greatly admired at the University for his unusual academic ability and was generously welcomed into the intimate fellowship of the then-distinguished professors of philosophy and mathematics. To cap off his "formal" education, at age 19 an honorary Master of Arts degree was conferred upon him. This carried with it a license to preach the gospel as a minister of the Scottish Established Church.

Of his brief pulpit episode, James Hogg, a colleague, wrote in a letter to Publisher James Fraser:

> ". . . he was licensed, but the first day he mounted the pulpit was the last — for he had then, if he has not still, a nervous something about him that made him swither when he heard his own voice and saw a congregation eyeing him; so he sticked his discourse, and vowed never to try that job again. It was a pity for the Kirk [the National Church of Scotland], . . . but it was a good day for Science . . . for if the doctor had gotten a manse, he might most likely have taken to his toddy like other folk."

This was in the year 1801. He immediately turned his great talents to the study of optics, and for twelve years conducted a series of experiments which were revealed to the public in "A Treatise Upon New Philosophical Instruments," published in 1813.

Brewster's treatise did not represent his only accomplishments during this period. In 1807, at the age of 26, the University of Aberdeen awarded him a Doctor of Letters degree, the highest literary distinction of that era, a truly unique achievement for one of his age. But this was not all; in 1808, he was elected a Fellow of the Royal Society of Edinburgh and the same year became editor of the Edinburgh Encyclopedia, a position he executed with excellence for more than 20 years.

In 1810 Brewster married Juliet McPherson, but scarcely anything is recorded of his family life. Shortly after his death, his daughter, a Mrs. Gordon, about whom little is known, published a biography entitled "The Home Life of Sir David Brewster." But reviewers determined that Mrs. Gordon's work contained more sentiment than analysis or fact and it was not considered authoritative.

It was in the year 1811, while writing an article on "Burning Instruments," that Brewster was led to investigate a theory of Buffon, which was to construct a lens of great diameter out of one piece of glass by cutting out the central parts in successive ridges like stair steps. Brewster did not consider Buffon's proposal practicable. However, it sparked an idea which produced awesome, scientific results. Thus was born an apparatus of then unequaled power — the construction of a lens by building it upon several circular segments. Here was a useful invention, later perfected, which produced the lighthouse as we know it, creating light-stabs of brilliance that pierced far into the night to guide mariners.

This breakthrough was followed by yet other honors. Brewster was admitted to the Royal Society of London and was later awarded the Rumford gold and silver medal for his theory on the polarization of light, which states that light reflected from a glass surface is completely polarized when the reflected and refracted rays are perpendicular to one another. Success followed success; and in 1816, the Institute of France adjudged him 3,000 francs — half the prizes — for the two most important scientific discoveries to have been made in the two previous years.

Then, as an added jewel to his already glittering optics crown, Brewster invented the kaleidoscope! This was the year 1816. Brewster was 35 years of age, and was already an established philosopher, writer, scientist and inventor. A copy of his patent is in the appendix.

engraved brass endpiece

Brewster's kaleidoscope created unprecedented clamor. In a history of Brewster's Kaleidoscope, found in the June 1818 volume of Blackwood's Magazine, Dr. Roget said:

> "In the memory of man, no invention, and no work, whether addressed to the imagination or to the understanding, ever produced such an effect. A universal mania for the instrument seized all classes, from the lowest to the highest, from the most ignorant, to the most learned, and every person not only felt, but expressed the feeling, that a new pleasure had been added to their existence."

But while Brewster was granted a patent, was acknowledged and acclaimed for his invention, he did not realize any monetary remuneration. Others did, however. There was some fault with the patent registration and before Brewster could claim any financial rewards, kaleidoscopes were quickly manufactured by aggressive entrepreneurs who sold hundreds of thousands with great financial success for themselves. Like so many other great men, this was to be the pattern of Brewster's life: great intellectual achievement without worldly compensation.

In 1823, the Institute of France elected Brewster a corresponding member. The Royal Academies of Russia, Prussia, Sweden and Denmark conferred upon him the highest distinctions accorded a foreigner. These high honors opened lines of communication for him with the great minds of Europe.

Antique Kaleidoscopes from around the globe

In mid-life, in 1832, he was knighted by William IV. This brought an instant social status that only those few touched by the King could know. But Brewster simply continued to pursue his investigations and experiments. In short, he remained the poorly paid teacher, the famous professor who James Hogg, in the same letter pictured thusly:

> "He has indeed some minor specialities about him. For example, he holds that soda water is wholesomer drink than bottled beer, objects to a body's putting a nipper of spirits in their tea, and maintains that you ought to shave every morning, and wash your feet every night — but who would wish to be severe on the eccentricities of genius?"

One of Brewster's most illustrious moments came in 1849. He was nominated as one of a panel of eight foreign associate nominees of the National Institute of France. So great were Brewster's achievements in comparison to all others that after examination, the Institute struck the names of all other candidates and Sir David Brewster stood in splendid isolation as the sole remaining candidate. His discoveries of the physical laws of metallic reflection and light absorption, of the optical properties of crystals and the law of the angle of polarization, along with his improvement of the stereoscope and lighthouse apparatus, surpassed most scientific achievements of that era.

It is for this man's contributions to philosophy and science that he is mainly remembered, but it was by his pen that he earned his living. In addition to editing the Edinburgh Encyclopedia from 1808 to 1830, he was one of the leading contributors to the 7th and 8th editions of the Encyclopedia Britannica, joint editor (1819-1824) of the Edinburgh Philosophic Journal, and then (1824-1832) editor of the Edinburgh Journal of Science. Among his most noteworthy separate publications should be mentioned his "Life of Sir Isaac Newton," "Letters to Sir Walter Scott on Natural Magic" and the "Martyrs of Science."

His lifelong love of nature's beauty, his abiding Christian faith and his ability to translate what he had learned into the written word in a way which could be understood even by children earned him the affection and respect of not only his associates and the populace of his time, but also of the generations which followed. One suspects that was all he ever really wanted.

It was during the Victorian age that the kaleidoscope reached its zenith. In those days it took longer for good news to travel, so while thousands were being manufactured all over Europe, it was not until the 1870's that kaleidoscopes found their way into American parlors.

Between the years of its introduction and the current rush of new innovations, many pounds of patents were granted, but only one kaleidoscope remains of any permanent significance — the Bush. Charles G. Bush of Boston manufactured a popular variety of parlor kaleidoscopes that have become valued collectors' items. These instruments have a barrel of banded black cardboard with a spoked brass wheel rotating an object cell, mounted on a turned wooden stand.

Most noteworthy about the Bush kaleidoscopes were the glass pieces contained in the object case. Bush had a basic mix of about 35 pieces, a third of which were liquid filled. Inside the liquids were air bubbles that continued to move even after the object case was at rest. Both the solid and the liquid-filled

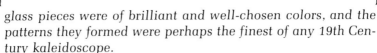

glass pieces were of brilliant and well-chosen colors, and the patterns they formed were perhaps the finest of any 19th Century kaleidoscope.

Bush secured several patents in 1873 and 1874; the first for the use of liquid-filled ampules in the object case; the second for a means to add and subtract pieces from the object case without having to disassemble it; one for the use of a color wheel as a backdrop for the images; and another for a four-legged wooden stand that could be disassembled for easier carrying and shipping. Excerpts from these patents appear in Appendix II on page 138.

It is hard to believe that this handsome instrument sold in those days for a mere $2.00. Today, if one can be found, it might go for as high as $1,000.

Section II

New Images Emerge

Kaleidoscope
Sparkling colors chase one another
Round and round in a circle of light
Symmetrical patterns of geodetic design
Mirror mandalas of image in flight.

New Images Emerge

The popularity of the kaleidoscope as entertainment for the whole family waned as the age of electronics advanced. Though they did continue to find their special place in Christmas stockings, kaleidoscopes remained for the most part, on the shelves of toy and novelty stores. It is only since the early 70's that new scopes with new images have spiraled onto the kaleidoscape with such renewed acceleration.

An article appearing in the November 1982 issue of Smithsonian Magazine did more to promote the kaleidoscope revival than any one thing. Jeanne McDermott's words and Wayne Sorce's photographs titillated the curiosity of some, nudged the nostalgia in others and impressed yet others with a double impact.

Brewster predicted his instrument would prove of the highest service in all the ornamental arts. It's doubtful though that he ever envisioned it becoming such a scintillating ornament of art itself.

While all the kaleidoscopes are composed of certain basic elements and the objective is the same — to project beautiful images — there are almost as many styles on the market as there are patterns in the scope. The original kaleidoscopes, and a few being made today, use a two-mirror system. Most, however, employ three mirrors and some use more than three. The basic difference is that two mirrors provide a reflection of the objects in the form of one image, centered and not multiplied. Three or more mirrors produce reflections of reflections so the patttern is duplicated to infinity.

Varying in price from under $5 to over $5,000, there is a kaleidoscope for every taste and budget. There are brass scopes, wooden scopes, acrylic, ceramic, even gold-plated and sterling silver scopes. Sizes range from miniature to man-size. Object cases are filled with hand-blown glass ampules, seashells, semi-precious stones, dried flowers, glass chips and baubles of all kinds. Rotating wheels are made of stained glass, gemstones, found objects and more. In some, the object case is a laticcino marble or a faceted crystal. Then there are scopes with polarized light, oil suspension scopes, electronic scopes, teleidoscopes and projector scopes. In short, a scope for all reasons, any season, and each one "pleasin'!"

The last twenty some-odd pages of Brewster's treatise are devoted to defending his authority as the true inventor of the kaleidoscope. One hundred and fifty years later, the same sort of defense may be heard from some of the modern designers.

With color vibrations astir in the atmosphere, and with such a renewal of enthusiasm for the instrument itself, it seems only natural that different people in different parts of the country are catching the same creative ideas at the same time.

Wouldn't it be great if all the energies spent disputing the originality of a design were put into constructive improvements and new endeavors? After all, there is room for everyone.

Howard Chesshire has a refreshing observation on the subject:

> "The credit for creativity should move more toward the viewer, rather than the artist. The creative design of kaleidoscopes is secondary, in my opinion, to the person's creative contact with his own environment while using kaleidoscopes."

One of the most difficult decisions has been the order of introduction of the artists who are designing today's multifaceted scopes. Consideration of chronology seemed logical; but after the first five or six, it became indeterminate. Arranging them by type proved just as difficult because one designer might make as many as 30 different types. Alphabetically by designers' names would appear a safe bet, yet many refer to scopes only by trade names. But arrangement by trademark or company name also proved equivocal since about a fourth of the artists refer to their craft as simply 'kaleidoscopes by . . . .'

I have opted to introduce the designers and their scopes to you at kaleido-random and hope they unfold in a meaningful pattern. (For an alphabetical listing of scope makers by name or trade name, please refer to index on pages 141-142). But first I want to explain a few words and terms you will encounter.

Kaleido-jargon

birefringent — doubly refracting material

cell — same as object case

dichromatic — glass showing different colors depending on the angle of light falling on it

diochroic — see dichromatic

disc — object case

first surface mirror — mirror is on the surface of the glass rather than behind as in a conventional mirror

flashed glass — one color of glass layered onto another color

front-surface mirror — same as first surface mirror

hot glass — *scrap glass that has been heated, fused and painted*

kaleidoscope — a tube-like instrument containing loose bits and pieces that are reflected by mirrors so that various symmetrical patterns appear as the instrument is rotated. The word kaleidoscope is derived from three Greek words meaning, beautiful-form-to see.

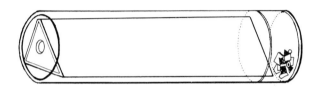

A basic kaleidoscope consists of an eye-piece, an object case containing objects to be viewed, a tube and either two or three mirrors along its length, angled toward each other.

The angle of the mirrors determines the number and complexity of the patterns. The pattern changes when the scope or object case is rotated.

laticcino — embedded threads of swirling white and colored glass

lens — *a piece of glass or other transparent substance with two curved surfaces, or one plane surface and one curved surface*

L.E.D. — light emitting diode

mandala — (muń-də-lə) a circular design containing concentric geometric forms, symbolizing the universe, totality or wholeness in Hinduism and Buddhism.

object case — container at end of scope holding objects to be viewed

oil-suspension scope — bits and pieces float in oil filled object case

optical treated mirror — chemically coated to prevent discoloration

polarized light — light that vibrates in one plane only (in contrast to ordinary light which vibrates in all directions)

shards — slivers of glass

slumped glass — flat glass heated until it takes a bent shape

teleidoscope — the object case is a lens. Whatever it is pointed towards is reflected again and again.

Karelitz Kaleidoscopes
Judith Karelitz

Forerunner in the surge of new images, with a patent granted in 1974, is New York artist, Judith Karelitz. Inspired by antique kaleidoscopes as a child, Judy determined that someday she was going to make the most beautiful kaleidoscope in the world. And she is convinced that she has done just that. No matter what artistic bent the scopes take, Judy is happy that she designed the very first modern plexiglass kaleidoscope utilizing polarized light.

Studying the very theories of light polarization advanced by Brewster, Judy probed and experimented until she realized her vision. "I was totally obsessed and possessed when I evolved the Karelitz Kaleidoscope," Judy admits. "I have never been so completely involved and dedicated in my life, and when in September of '71, the Karelitz Kaleidoscope appeared at The New York Museum of Modern Art, it was like a dream come true."

Totally today in structure, yesterday in appeal and tomorrow in concept, the exterior of this limited signed edition of 100, is as unique as the interior. Tall and sleek, the clear column of plexiglass contains a hollow red transparent prism instead of mirrors. Colorless pieces of doubly refracting material ebb and flow in fluid, creating imagery that is distinctly different from any other scopes anywhere. Since no colored glass is used, only polarized light, the colors are different too. Purples and magentas float in and out of soft pastels.

Here is the way Judy describes it: "Ordinary white light which vibrates in all directions is polarized along one plane when it passes through the base of the tube. The light then enters clear, colorless pieces of birefringent material and is reorganized by the eye-piece to produce the startling colors that you see. These color combinations are completely unique, except, perhaps sometimes one might see such colors in a garden — but with more opacity."

At the request of The Museum of Modern Art, Judy developed the Karascope, a patented, inexpensive variation of her limited edition. Karascope I proved such a success that the Smithsonian Institute in Washington, D.C. commissioned a Karascope II. These two designs, produced in large numbers, remain two of her most popular models. They are sold in museums and shops across the country, along with her newer Signature and Summer editions.

An outstanding feature inherent in Judy's polarized light scopes, and exclusively hers, is the turning mechanism. With a twist of the end piece, the design changes. Turn the eye piece and only the colors change. Turn them both and voila! the interior world changes. Asymmetrical images of the spectral colors of light itself, drift and float like billowing clouds and undulating rainbows. They are in marked contrast to the more traditional geometric symmetry viewed in the average scope.

Another special characteristic of the Karelitz scopes is their ability to shine on cloudy days. Most kaleidoscopes are activated by the sun or artificial light, but for viewing polarized light scopes, gray skies are even better than blue.

Judy's award-winning sculpture and photographs convey her intimate sense of nature. As she puts it, "In my work I have tried to encapsulate my deep connection with nature by translating the natural and physical phenomena found there — water, sky, ocean, earth, rainbows, flowers, pebbles, rocks — into mutable self-contained forms. I like to think of my involvement with nature as a joining — as though I am putting my signature on nature."

When I asked Judy what she had in mind for the future, she said "I'm working on several different prototypes and I think you are going to be pleased, especially with some very feathery optical effects." Then she added, "As long as I can remember, I've visualized a tall scope like the Karelitz Kaleidoscope which would project images on the ceiling. I would still love to create such a sculpture."

And no doubt she will, because this talented sculptress, photographer and artist is a true master of light, shape and color.

Kaleidoscopes by
Dorothy Marshall

About the same time that Judy Karelitz was packaging polarized light into cardboard tubes and blazing the plexiglass trail, Dorothy Marshall was busy pioneering the return of the hand-crafted cottage industry kaleidoscope. Her company was originally called Oz Optics.

"Nobody was selling truly hand-made scopes when I started," Dorothy explains. "I made each piece myself and then took them to shows and sold them, and they weren't easy to sell either, because people in those days thought of a kaleidoscope as a cheap toy — not a quality art form."

Dorothy's life was as varied and colorful as the images she began producing: a stint as a construction worker, summer theatre in Vermont, training show birds in Florida (the large parrots would ride bicycles and skate!). Through it all she managed to log about 30,000 miles hitchhiking around the country.

It was while tutoring learning-disabled children in the early 70's that Dorothy hit upon the idea to recreate one of her favorite childhood toys — a kaleidoscope. She had the kids construct scopes using toilet paper tubes for the casing. Later she made scopes for gifts using better materials; and before she knew it, she was in business.

Coming a long way from those empty paper tubes, all of Dorothy's quality scopes are made of solid hardwood casings banded with polished brass, complete with high curvature lenses, safety eyepieces and accessible interiors.

Dorothy makes a crystal scope which uses a full-lead Austrian crystal for the object cell. One luxury model is an 11-inch cylinder of black walnut ringed with sterling silver. She also makes an oil-scope which creates "slow and relaxing patterns" as stained glass chips float about in an oil-filled cartridge, and a teleidoscope wherein a lens is substituted for the object case.

Perhaps the most distinctive characteristic of Dorothy's work

25

is the thought and care she devotes to the structural design. A sheet of instructions is packaged with each scope explaining its care and repair, just one more facet of thoughtfulness she injects into her work.

"Kaleidoscopes are intended to be handled, shared and passed down," she says. "I know that I am creating tomorrow's heirlooms, and that knowledge determines my choice of design and materials, and my dedication to the highest quality of handcrafting."

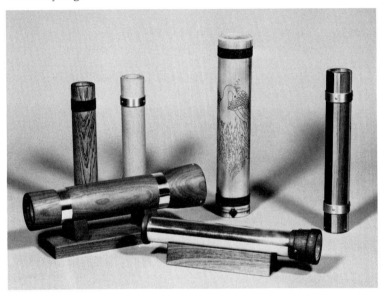

Mandala Kaleidoscopes
Howard Chesshire

Howard Chesshire had an idea for a special kaleidoscope. It was only after experimenting with mirrors and lenses for four years that he learned Sir David Brewster had tested and proved such an instrument more than 150 years earlier. But that didn't bother Howard. He is glad that he didn't realize the telescopic kaleidoscope, as it was originally termed, was already in existence. He had the personal thrill and pleasure of discovering this mandala machine for himself in 1973.

Chesshire strongly believes that the teleidoscope is the purest form of any type of kaleidoscope. "My lens-equipped scope gives the viewer the ability to compose his own image and to change and control it," he says. "I find it particularly gratifying that my artform will continue to create new images and new art even after it leaves my studio."

"The ultimate value of my kaleidoscope is the potential each viewer has to see the artistic value in his own environment," Howard explains. Pointing his scope at a bowl of fresh eggs in his Vermont farm kitchen, Howard told me to look carefully. "Open your other eye," he insisted. "You don't have to close one eye and squint when viewing nature's kaleidoscope."

Chesshire's in good company with his preference for the teleidoscope. He showed me pages 81-85 of the 1858 revised edition of Brewster's Treatise on the Kaleidoscope.

"Without such an extension of power, (referring to the substitution of a lens in place of a cell) the kaleidoscope might only be regarded as an instrument of amusement; but when it is made to embrace objects of all magnitudes, and at all distances, it takes its place as a general philosophical instrument, and becomes of the greatest use in the fine, as well as the useful arts . . .

The patterns which are thus presented to the eye are essentially different from those exhibited by the simple kaleidoscope. Here the objects are independent of the observer, and all their movements are represented with the most singular effect in the symmetrical picture, which is as much superior to what is given by the simple instrument, as the sight of living or moving objects is superior to an imperfect portrait of them."

The Mandala Kaleidoscope contains windows, mirrors, lenses, a prism, and discrete space. The three fine double convex lenses project an image of any object upon the mirrors. Then the image multiples as it travels through the prism, producing more than 200 reflections of the object in symmetrical patterns. It transforms the objects from your own surroundings into a kinetic montage of vibrant images and inspiring designs. The visual potential is as infinite as the colors and shapes around you.

While Mandala Kaleidoscopes come in only one model, they wear many "dresses," as the Chesshire's three-year old daughter Crystal calls the exterior coverings of suedecloth, leather, marbelized paper or cork.

27

Crystal helping "dress" Mandala scopes

Howard and Faye gave me permission to print their wedding vows. This meaningful document reveals clearly how their lives are totally intertwined with the Mandala.

I have loved you since I met you,
And I now know that I will love you forever.
We are Northern Lights
My Mirror, My Mandala, Our Art

This is the threshold
Beyond is the calm of knowing forever;
Growing together —
Living and loving together forever

I will hold your head, heart, hands and health
I will feel and massage your body.
I will excite your mind.
I will fulfill your expectations.

I will create rainbows in your showers.
I will create crystals in your snow.
I will create color in your sunshine.
I will embroider your lifelight with glow.

We have spun our certainty,
Found our faith and lost our fears.
We will become a circle,
A unity to float through all the years —
My life is ours — a mandala.

Windseye
Doug Johnson

Creating from images that well up from his inner experiences, Doug Johnson was not only a precursor in the kaleidoscope explosion, he is an innovative designer who was the first to introduce many of the styles and concepts being embellished today.

He remembers that as a child, he fell in love with the remnants of a local industry — costume jewelry. The brightly colored glass and plastic that frequently dusted the sidewalks captured his attention. So did the stained glass windows in church "where my mind wandered . . . enjoying the music and admiring the colors . . . , " he reminisces.

These were just the beginnings of an aesthetic awareness for Doug, whose formal background of math, psychology and computer science has come back full circle to that of color and image.

It was only a matter of time until Doug merged his scientific world into his colorful dream world. More than ten years ago while working with computers, he visited a local arts and crafts show. An exhibit of stained glass recaptured his early fascination. He saw a way of living the dreams he loved while at the same time creating something tangible. By 1977, Doug abandoned computers and worked full-time with stained glass. In 1978, he came out with his first kaleidoscope. He and his wife Dottie now own and operate a beautiful high-quality arts and crafts shop in Florida, where he continues to create new scopes.

"I find that I am happiest working with images . . . I share this with the world. People can move into a visual space that is relaxing and calming. The real value in a kaleidoscope is refreshment."

Doug takes great pride in his special contributions to the growing art of kaleidoscopy, and rightly so. His influence and list of "firsts" is impressive.

As Doug points out, his early method of combining kevels (his own term for his copyrighted glass object cases) with elongated triangular mirrored bodies soldered with copper, may not seem so distinctive now that many others are employing the same technique. Realizing that the inner image is the most crucial part of a scope, Doug was among the first to use front surface mirrors in all his designs.

First to use clear and beveled glass for the bodies of the scope, he then designed and developed the kevel, using stained glass materials and techniques. One of his innovations was a kevel that could be opened, thus enabling "each person to control his own kaleidoscope experience," by putting in special objects and favorite colors. For even more variety, Doug introduced interchangeable kevels and wheels, and double combinations thereof.

This ability to "personalize" the kaleidoscope to the viewer's liking is important to Doug since he wants people to be able to sample and enjoy as much of the infinite variety of styles, textures and colors as possible.

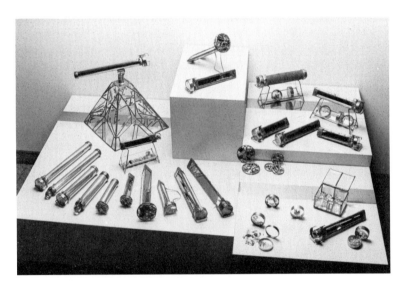

To his credit also goes the first marble scope. By rotating high quality laticcino marbles at the end of the tube, streams of color bounce off the inner mirrors to create myriad patterns. New on the market is his adapter which accommodates a range of various sized marbles in the same scope.

Highly original and singularly his own, the binocular kaleidoscope joins two viewers which focus on one set of wheels. Doug has two versions of this bi-scope, one of which includes a special mirror which allows pastel tinted images to enter the visual field through the body of the scope. The blending of these images with those entering through the end piece creates extremely sophisticated and multi-dimensional images of extraordinary colors — it's like a technicolor map of fairyland. This he calls his "Super Binoc."

Maximizing the kaleidoscope's playfulness, Doug offers more than 30 different sizes, shapes and styles. The body of one model is made of slumped glass. This technique involves heating glass until it bends and assumes the shape of the mold on which it has been placed in the kiln. The bits and pieces in the kevel are torch-worked. This whole process is quite new and the results are astonishing. And he's not through yet. A simple prism scope is another new product. Containing no mirrors, it is just a solid triangle of glass with a rotating marble for the end piece. Without the marble, it is a prism which breaks down white light into the spectral colors of the rainbow.

Referring again to the images, Doug says "Images in kaleidoscopes are non-verbal, not linked to words, or to anything at all. They are invitations to go off into other lands where no one else is . . . they are private spaces, creative realms of intrigue . . ."

C. Bennett Scopes
Carolyn Bennett

By studying "How a Young Lad Can Make a Kaleidoscope From a Tin," in an old "Book of Knowledge," a young lassie was launched on her scope-making career. Most children are intrigued with kaleidoscopes at one time or another, but then they are tossed aside for a new diversion. Carolyn Bennett never lost the initial fascination.

She remembers at age eight, visiting the Corning Glass factory where in a choice between two souvenirs, she passed up a kaleidoscope in favor of a trinket. She kept wishing she had opted for the kaleidoscope. Of course, the story has a happy ending, for Carolyn did eventually find another kaleidoscope. She is still finding them, this time on her own drawing board, and you can find them in shops and galleries all across the land.

Carolyn studied fine arts in college and graduate school. Her work reflected the symmetrical images she observed through the teleidoscope. How she wished there were a camera that could photograph those geometric designs so that she could draw and paint from the photos.

Even while Carolyn was teaching art, she always kept on the look-out for tubes — transferring any she could find into scopes. The more she made, the more she wanted to make. Finally, Carolyn resigned her teaching position to do what she loved most — making kaleidoscopes. She reviewed the directions in that article she had read as a child and began making scopes with the intention of taking photographs through them.

By persevering with the photographic aspect that originally intrigued Carolyn, she has now developed a Scopelens™ which enables one to photograph the world as seen through a teleidoscope. Or by filling the lens with any desired item, the vivid interiors of a kaleidoscope itself can be photographed.

"Just as there is an ever expanding world awaiting new paintings and sculpture, I believe there is an expanding audience for kaleidoscopes," Carolyn explains. From tiny "little jewels"

32

that can be worn around the neck, to six-foot outdoor scopes, and from romantic hearts and flowers to streamlined high-tech, C. Bennett Scopes offers more than twenty styles.

Carolyn's prolific output is equalled only by her positive outlook. "There is a very mystical and personal experience happening when a person looks through a kaleidoscope," she says. "Although I place the colors in the chamber, it is the viewer who controls the scope with his own karma. He steps into his own private world of vision and only he sees, feels, and understands that moment. I feel blessed that I have been able to share with people something beautiful that may be inspirational to them."

Acrylic is the material Carolyn prefers to work with, finding it sturdily transparent, without being fragile. But it is the crystal quality permitting illusion beyond illusion that captures her imagination. Two of her most popular scopes, "Crystal Vision" and "Infinity" use an acrylic ball that acts as a lens to convert the acrylic cylinder into a teleidoscope.

"I like to think of scope-making as a perfect combination of many art forms," Carolyn says. "When I mix pieces of glass inside a scope, it is like painting. When I design the exterior, it is sculpture." She hand paints some of her scopes and coordinates the colors inside. In others she floats seashells in a clear liquid. And new waters were charted when Carolyn introduced the kaleidoscope as a wearable art form. One necklace scope is made of sterling silver filled with semi-precious stones.

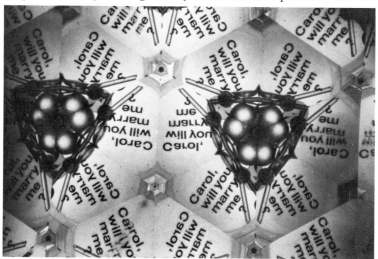

Customized and personalized scopes are popular items at C. Bennett Scopes. Counted among its commissions are large industrial organizations, children's museums, and amusement parks. Recently there was a request for one with a very special message. Looking inside this surprise scope, the recipient read the words, "Will you marry me?" Evidently the results were positive, because there are more message scopes in the works.

The Symphonoscope, designed as a fund raiser for the Women's Committee of the National Symphony Orchestra, is a beauty. A sheet of music wraps around the tube with music notes, violins and a French horn tumbling about with coordinated color pieces inside.

Versatility and variety are definitely a scopemark of C. Bennett Scopes. "The infinite possibilities inherent in kaleidoscopes continue to inspire my creative forces and excite me daily. Actually," Carolyn admits, "my dream goal is to produce the world's largest kaleidoscope, one that people would be able to walk through so that they might experience the ultimate kaleidoscope image."

Kaleidovisions
Peach Reynolds

Peach Reynolds is responsible for one of the most exciting developments of all — the world's first electronic kaleidoscope. This battery-operated high-tech electrascope is activated by sound. By simply pointing it in the direction of any sound source, you can see a miniature display of fireworks. Try some marching-band music or Beethoven's Fifth Symphony and watch those flashing L.E.D.'s really jump.

"A kaleidoscope is a lot like life," says Cary Peach Reynolds, one of the most well-known names in the kaleidoworld, "it offers beauty, fantasy, stillness, motion, surprise. It suggests planning and order; it is random and unpredictable." As one of the first to turn his hobby into a successful business, Peach has been turning out a prolific array of hand-crafted, high quality scopes for more than ten years. He was also among the first to use front-surfaced, optical quality mirrors in all of his scopes, assuring crisper, crystal clear images with every turn. "It has at last become an art form accepted by the art establishment," he asserts happily, "so now there is a lot of room for development."

Reynolds, who makes his home in Texas and calls his business Kaleidovisions, speaks of his entry into the field as an "unplanned adventure." Several years ago, he discovered an old kaleidoscope at a friend's house and thought it would be nice to own one. Since he couldn't find one and couldn't find a book of instructions, he "felt" his way; and, through trial and error, he blazed his own trail to success. Many thousand scopes later, he still contends that each and every kaleidoscope is an experiment unto itself.

Kaleidovisions produces several basic designs but the changing pattern of form, color, texture and light brought about by paper clips, comb teeth, seashells, jewelry, filigree, mardigras beads, stained glass, buttons, sequins and colored oils makes each one individual and exciting. Their "see-through" turns the world into a kaleidoscope. Oil suspension models are made with either colored objects or a variety of tiny sea shells drifting

35

in a clear oil. Colors in his polarascope are formed by polarized light and take on a geometric appearance, while three colors of oil intermingle to create the illusion of an artist's canvas in the aquascope. There is even a camerascope which screws onto any camera, allowing one to capture on film a kaleidoscope scene of one's choice. The large tubular bodies of a great many of Peach's scopes are handpainted with swirls of color making them easy to recognize. He also makes some with exotic natural woods.

For the overwhelmed and indecisive, there is a handsome darkwood partitioned case which holds one kaleidoscope with six interchangeable end pieces. Or, if someone wants a more personalized scope, Peach will create a special one in which the customer's favorite trinkets and treasures — say a petal from an old corsage or a baby's tooth — can be forever immortalized. And, there is just no telling what innovations he will have come up with by the time you read this book. To quote Peach: "Not even the sky is the limit."

Van Dyke, Ltd.

Craig Musser   Bill O'Connor

Certainly, if there were an Academy Award category for kaleidoscopes, Van Dyke, Ltd. would be nominated and might well walk away with top honors for both its Series II and III.

Hailed by one ardent collector as the "Rolls-Royce" of scopes and referred to in Smithsonian Magazine as the "ultimate" kaleidoscope, Series II is no longer available. A limited edition of fifty was a sellout at $3,800 a scope.

A 19th Century Bush scope served as inspiration for the Van Dyke masterpiece. While studying Buddhism in India, Craig Musser realized the similarity of kaleidoscope patterns to the Mandala designs used in meditation. At first he thought the Bush instrument could not be improved upon, but it slowly occurred to him that there had to be optical quality mirrors available in today's market that were not available a hundred years ago. Moreover, to add sophisticated and intricate glass objects and more imaginative colors, one could transform the kaleidoscope of old into a magnificent modern treasure. In his quest for the best, he set out to find a superior glass blower and this quest led him to Bill O'Connor.

O'Connor first sculpted with wood, but as he sat in his earliest glass-blowing class with Josh Simpson, he knew that he had found his true medium. The "roar of the furnace, the smell of the glass" struck a responsive chord. The process seemed to blend with his personality and he went about building his own furnaces which, when completed, produced enough energy to heat his entire house.

Perceiving the moon to be night's mirror, Bill's colors run the spectrum from glittering shadows of evening through the faint blush of dawn, bursting into the full radiance of day. Each handblown, lamp-worked tiny glass object is a work of art unto itself, a wee sculpture assuming an exotic shape. There are minarets, shepherds' crooks, horses' manes, lightning bolts, even a unicorn's horn. The finest pieces are filled with oils, mica or other tiny colored glass bits to achieve an added dimension of movement. Thirty to forty of these exquisite objects tumble about in the object case, accounting for the dazzlingly spectacular images.

Clockwise rotation of the brass wheels produce patterns that form from the center, outward. Counter-clockwise rotation produces more ornate designs which flow from the outer edges, inward. Whichever way the wheels are turned, one sees tinted poetry in motion. A projection lamp, also made of solid brass, is attached to the same elegantly finished hardwood base, complete with an engraved plaque. Indeed, in the Series II, the magic and nostalgia of the Victorian Bush scope endures, but the images change and advance to a zenith of perfection unparalleled.

Series III changes direction in style, but not in quality or optics. Stunningly sleek and modern in design, this handsome instrument rests in its own wooden, oblong, leather-lined stand. It is a limited edition of 350, each signed and numbered. A built-in recessed bronze dial controls the image, presenting an optimum illusion in a minimal space . . . for while the glass pieces are smaller, they are more intricate and the images are seen behind a hand-faceted glass lens.

Series III

Craig Musser agrees with other scope makers and scope lovers that there is a quality of magic in a good kaleidoscope, that "from a random jumble of pieces an infinite number of never-repeating, stunningly-beautiful images can arise. No other art form possesses this unique combination of unpredictability and new beauty being generated from the destruction of the preceding form."

The spiritual as well as the magical comes into view. Musser says, "I sometimes experience a renewal of spirit when I look into a kaleidoscope. I am reminded of such basic principles as the ever changing quality of the universe, the necessity for destruction of the old to generate the new, the complete unpredictability of existence and the underlying order that is inhumanly beautiful."

Craig Musser and Bill O'Connor, two gifted and inspired people, have created kaleidoscopes that will "live" as a standard of excellence.

Laughing Coyote
Ron and Claudia Lee

For many years the Lees of the Laughing Coyote had been creating a variety of contemporary wooden items which incorporated flowers and weeds. One day a customer asked if they could make a kaleidoscope with flowers and they were immediately embarked on a new venture. They soon discovered that their customers showed greater interest in scopes than any of their other products.

The Laughing Coyote's representation in the scope field indicates that they have met their objectives: beauty and quality at affordable prices. Ron and Claudia continue to experiment, adding new models on a regular basis.

One of the most original is a musical kaleidoscope. A vertical viewing tube is attached to a platform which contains a music box. A small pewter dish to hold colored items of your choice revolves as the music plays. Ron says when he planned this scope he visualized a Victorian parlor object. Well, the Mozart tune and slowly revolving dried petals and bits of ribbon and beads have a Victorian flavor. But the sleek lines of his inlaid ebony and the overall outward appearance is quite 20th Century, making a beautiful and appropriate blend of then and now.

The floral scope continues to be one of the most popular of their line. Ron executes the wonderful hardwood cases and Claudia takes care of the flowers which are dried and then cast in a resin compound. Some of the wheels contain delicate ferns and Queen Ann's Lace. Others are filled with rose petals and pansies or wildflowers along with tiny Victorian faces, fans and other bits of nostalgia. Wheels are interchangeable so you can collect your own scope garden.

The Lees derive great satisfaction from public reaction to their scopes, especially children. Two items that remain perennial favorites are geared to children: the Kidoscope, a small wooden scope with a leather carrying strap that looks like a sling shot, and the Treasure Scope, an upright scope which

comes with a covered "viewer dish" and a bag of "tumbles" (dried flowers, stones and assorted colorful trinkets). The fun is being able to substitute your own shells, jewels or other trinkets.

Rose Marie Raccioppi uses this particular scope in her treatment of brain-injured children. As president of the New York Association for the Learning Disabled, she has this to say about the Treasure Scope. "It allows one to change the materials to be viewed. I plan to encourage my students to collect memorable pieces from a happening of their choice. With thoughts of the original happening, they will view their memorable pieces to create a new kaleidoscopic experience. Creative descriptions of their recollected experience will be developed and accompanied by descriptions of their newly created kaleidoscopic view."

Dean Kent   Stephen Auger

Northampton Studios
Stephen Auger
Dean Kent

As an artist, Stephen Auger was creating paintings which explored the harmonic relationship between light and color long before he discovered Brewster's formula and designs for kaleidoscopes.

Always a plodder, Stephen pounded the pavements of New York City, hauling his portfolio, trying to get introduced to people who could appreciate his work. To make ends meet, he painted fabrics for fashion designers. It was while he was so occupied that he met Gene Moore, the man who had been designing Tiffany's windows for thirty years. Moore permitted Auger to place five paintings in Tiffany's windows and he sold them all.

Scopes proved a natural for Stephen, whose other interests include physics and optics. Combining his artist's eye for color and form with a scientist's passion for precision, Stephen has developed a very special series of kaleidoscopes.

The Auger Collection is a one-of-a-kind, acid etched solid brass kaleidoscope available in four sizes, with each one signed, dated and numbered. Semi-precious stones and liquified glass drawn into spirals, loops and whimsical shapes form the basis for the gorgeous visions which indeed rival a royal treasure chest. By simply rotating the object case you enter a world of enchanting mille fleur imagery — a full orchestra of color in a capsule.

When I read the brochure describing Stephen's new "Parlor Kaleidoscope," I phoned immediately to order one, sight unseen. When it was delivered I was delighted beyond telling. It was all the brochure promised. I don't believe his words can be improved upon, so here they are verbatim.

Exquisitely realized and beautifully crafted, this American Parlor Kaleidoscope quietly explodes in an intense orchestration of images. Brilliant colors are brought together in stellar patterns of infinite intricate complexity. The rotating object case holds sparkling treasures, delicately shaped glass and semi-precious crystals. Each piece is carefully chosen and collected to produce harmonic cadences of

41

color. The resultant, radiant play is endlessly changing and utterly seductive in the magic of its vivid timbre.

Equally beautiful is the object itself. Precision machined and painstakingly assembled by hand, this kaleidoscope will be treasured for generations. Adjustable and of solid brass on a walnut base, each surface is polished and detailed, each material glowing in its own patina. Measuring twelve inches high and twelve inches long, this American Parlor Kaleidoscope has an authoritative presence equal to the splendor that its images convey."

From the engraved eye piece with its optically ground magnifying lens, through the precision-cut float glass mirrors, to the random tumbling gems in the "wheeling" object cell, Stephen and his partner, Dean Kent, have created state-of-the-art optical instruments that are truly "jewelry for the mind."

There are more varieties of the 2-wheel kaleidoscope than of any other type. You can find giant wheels, miniature wheels, glass wheels, agate wheels, a combination of agate and glass, acrylic wheels, wheels embedded with dried flowers, gem encrusted wheels, and even gear-powered wheels.

As if that isn't enough wheels to keep you turning, I've come up with an idea for a variation that makes a dazzling addition to the whirling scope. Simply drill a hole in the middle of two holograms, or dimension discs, glue them back-to-back and then attach it to your favorite 2-wheeler. You'll be amazed — although the hologram is not transparent, if enough space if left between the end piece and the wheel so that the light can play on it — wow! I'm not going to apply for a patent, but please when you are playing with one, refer to it as a Cozyscope!

MS Designs
Susan Stover

Susan Stover of MS Designs was one of the very first to utilize two wheels as the object case for a kaleidoscope. And she did it in a big way — really big. Susan built a five-foot tall oak tripod and placed on top is a walnut barreled scope with two stained glass wheels. Unusual in both design and dimension, it proved popular when it appeared in 1978 and remains a good seller today.

When Nieman Marcus and a toy shop on Rodeo Drive in Beverly Hills bought that and the rest of her line, Susan knew she had a winner and she hasn't attempted to make any new models. That doesn't mean she won't, however. Meanwhile, kaleidoscopes are only a small part of the wood and glass inventory at MS Designs.

Collector Pat Seaman looking through large MS Designs Scope

Classical Glass
Peg and Dennis Comeau

Peg and Dennis Comeau of Classical Glass have come up with a couple different twists to a basic wood and glass two-wheel kaleidoscope. Hexagon, cone-shaped viewing tubes are made of oak or walnut, lined with six mirrors, and each scope stands on it's own built-in foot. Two varying sized color glass wheels spin freely on these hardwood cones. Wheels on other scopes are usually of identical size. This variation, though slight, really gives a different look — quite attractive. Textures and colors are different too.

Classical Glass also makes a very special edition which is an extremely large version of their standard scope. Each one is an individually designed one-of-a-kind piece constructed in a variety of select woods. Peg says this model is especially popular with the men.

"Our business is a family one in which friends and relatives help out from time to time. The lifestyle that we are able to lead by living in the country inspires our creativity in bringing visual pleasure to others by way of our scopes. Each time we sell a kaleidoscope to someone, it's like making a new friend — they feel we've put a little joy in their lives, and they take home a part of us in the scope."

Chesnik-Koch, Ltd.
Janice Chesnick
Sheryl Koch

Appearing on the scope scene earlier than most, with perhaps the largest production of all two-wheel glass and brass scopes, is the mother-daughter team known as Chesnik-Koch, Ltd. Actually, the team is comprised of four players, because each of the husbands represents an active part of this kaleidoscope enclave. "When we say 'Kaleidoscopes by Chesnik-Koch' we mean all four of us," says Janice Chesnik who was the first in the family to adopt the scope as a way of living.

Janice has been toying with colors since her first crayons. The simple kaleidoscope she owned as a child added impetus to her hobby and her interest in color design. Years later, while attending the University of Kansas, she took a few art courses which gave vent to her creativity through a variety of handcrafts. A move to California, marriage, two daughters and many crafts later, Janice found her true niche, when she incorporated her stained glass knowledge and experience into the stained-glass kaleidoscope.

She found being able to create colors and patterns that moved and changed enthralling and, at the same time, she had found a way to turn her leisure-time activity into a profit-making business at home.

When the orders started rolling in and her confidence grew, Janice shared her enthusiasm and know-how with her daughter, Sheryl Koch, who lives in Colorado.

Together and apart, this mother-daughter team has grown successful and renowned in the kaleidoscope field. They make many adaptations of one basic 2-wheel scope. Two sets of wheels are available with each style. One is made of German antique stained glass complemented by a secondary wheel of textured glass. The other version uses the finest Brazilian agates in the primary wheel.

Chesnik's scopes tend to be contemporary in style with her use of black acrylic, sleek chromium and blond and colored leathers. Koch's models veer toward the traditional with the use of oak in her pedestals, tripods and boxes. One whimsical design Sheryl came out with is the Bathscope.

The firm Chesnik-Koch represents more than the fulfillment of a dream. It is a strong family bond, soldered with mutual love and respect.

Bits of the Past
Irene and Bill Ecuyer

Small wheels can cast sparkling shadows. One of the trimmest and lightest scopes to be found, originates in the Vermont home of Irene and Bill Ecuyer. Its calming effect has proven practical application. The Ecuyer's dentist keeps one in his office for patients to enjoy before undergoing treatment.

Before retiring, Bill was making stained glass lamps and boxes as a hobby. Kaleidoscopes had always interested him, and with more time to experiment, he turned his attention to creating a scope that was in his own words, "different."

Working side by side, Irene and Bill produce two models. One has a wheel with 12 colors and the other contains 24. Making them entirely by hand, they cut the mirrors, cast the old lineotype metal wheels and even use their own lathe. After shaping and sealing the 1 x 9½ inch vinyl pieces with heat, they sand and paint them with three coats of flat black paint. Deep rich colors are then embedded in resin.

Spinning smoothly and swiftly, the tiny wheels produce miniature images reminiscent of darkly stained glass windows found in ancient cathedrals.

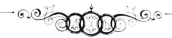

Kaleidoscopes by
Carrie Souza

"We are all rainbows," says Carrie Souza, kaleidoscope maker based in Hawaii. "Colors are a vital part of our being and we can't help being affected by them — physically, emotionally, mentally, for our healing, creativity and spirituality."

Carrie makes a large triangular iridescent stained glass scope with an inlaid pattern of contrasting iridized glass. One design is a six-pointed star and another is a pyramid with sun rising. Each of the two wheels contains eighteen pieces of stained glass, which revolve on ball bearings. The brass rods on which the wheels spin are threaded so that the discs can be removed easily for cleaning and interchanging. Seashells are placed between the discs to enhance the patterns. A small bit of mirror is tucked among the pieces so occasionally you might get a surprising glimpse of your own eye.

Like most scope artisans, Carrie Souza believes that the kaleidoscope serves many purposes: to relax, to stimulate, to exercise the imagination, to invite meditation and to teach children color blending and shading. She also feels it serves as a good tool for communication. In fact, Carrie's romance with the scope inspired her to pen these lines:

> "Kaleidoscopes are works of art which attune to our very being.
> Just go inside for one moment and let your mind absorb the colors,
> For they are the blessings of light."

P-BAR-K Productions
Kirk Webber

You can almost taste the colors as the wheels spin on Kirk Webber's hot glass kaleidoscope. And you can feel the silken grain in the bodies of his scopes which are fashioned from exotic woods such as aspen, Indian rosewood, padauk, cherry, walnut and oak. Some have rich inlays, creating contrasting artistic patterns.

When I mentioned to Kirk how sensational I found the effects of the hot glass in his scopes, he told me that Jeff Kuykendall, a glass blower, provides him with the scrap glass and glass rods which are heated with a blow torch, fused and then painted. According to Kirk, he is the only scope maker incorporating hot-glass into his designs.

Some of his wheels contain brightly colored wild flowers. A special 24-hour process used for dyeing the flowers leaves the brilliant colors intact, thus enhancing the imagery. Another unusual P-Bar-K scope is a large chunky square model banded with leather and using a lead crystal for the object case.

Kirk is the first to admit that while he enjoys the images inside his scopes, it is the wood used for the bodies as well as the patterns and textures he can achieve that really capture his fancy.

48

Clockwise from top left: Karalitz
Karascope II©, The Auger Kaleidoscope, Antique Bush, Stained Glass
by Karadimos, C. Bennett Scopes©,
and VanCort, the Classic.

Private antique kaleidoscope collection

Brewster scope with interchangeable object cells.

Antique cane kaleidoscope   Brewster scope in original box

Rare antique kaleidoscope brought $5000 at London auction

From two private collections of antique kaleidoscopes

Van Dyke, Series II

Hand-blown ampules

Karalitz Kaleidoscope, Limited Edition

Prototypes of new Karalitz scopes

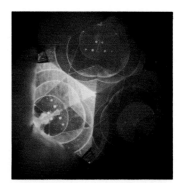

Karalitz Kaleidoscope©

Karalitz Signature edition©

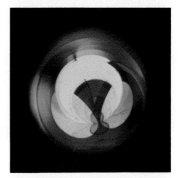

Karalitz Karascope©

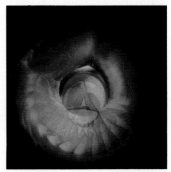

Karalitz new scope©

Doug Johnson kaleidoscopes photographed at New Morning Gallery

C. Bennett Scopes

Chesnik-Koch Kaleidoscopes

Large outdoor model by Dorothy Marshall

Kaleidoscopes by Peach Reynolds

Kaleidoscopes by Carrie Souza

Fantasy Glass by Lesley

Bits of the Past

Classical Glass

Kaleidoscopes by Dee Potter

Kaleidoscopes by Tom Proctor

Mandala Kaleidoscopes

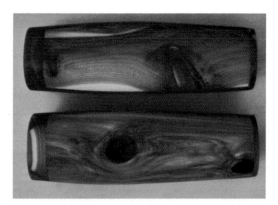

Working Wood Kaleidoscopes

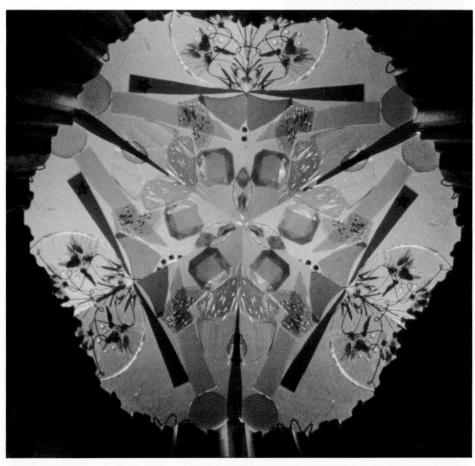

P-BAR-K Productions

Kaleidoscopes by Corki Weeks

One of a kind kaleidoscope
by Rick Palosky

Gallocolley Glass
Carmen and Stephen Colley

Wheel scopes take a new turn at the Gallocolley Glass studio. Glitter, dazzle, drama and surprises are embedded right along with a profusion of gemstones, Austrian crystals, antique buttons, fused glass and faceted jewels. It is the "found objects," however, which provide the piece de resistance to these original klajescopes (collage-a-scopes). Found objects are treasures that have been found or collected through the years, or may be unusual pieces that have a special personal meaning. The inclusion of so many beautiful objects adds infinite variations of color and elaborate patterns beyond the wildest imagination.

Carmen Colley fell in love with kaleidoscopes at age seven when she traded her favorite yo-yo for a scope. The idea of creating her own version, however, did not occur to her until a few years ago when she ran across a marble scope. She was delighted with this novel variation of the scope and decided she could produce one even more beautiful. She set out to do just that, and with great results.

In their San Antonio garage studio, Carmen and her architect husband, Stephen, make a couple of simple versions. But it is their singularly deluxe double-wheeler that attracts the most attention and that they find emotionally fulfilling.

One of the Colley's numerous finishing touches is a kaleidoscope kozy. This is a Shibori drawstring bag, hand dyed by Marquetta Johnson to harmonize with the colors in the scope. To cap it off, Stephen hand-paints a Certificate of Content, which details the magic recipe contained in each individually-named scope.

Carmen is so caught up in her scopes that she almost hates to part with each new "child." But when the buyer's enthusiasm matches hers, then it's a different story and she is doubly thrilled. The magic that she feels in kaleidoscopes is visually translated into each treasure created at Gallocolley Glass.

Kaleidoscopes by
Tom Proctor

Tom makes a smooth ceramic scope with bright acrylic wheels. "Just as mother Earth is a sphere in constant change, so is the kaleidoscope," says Tom Proctor. "With each new turn there is a new discovery."

Tom might be considered by some as a newcomer to the kaleidoscene, but he is certainly not new to the art world. His life has revolved around a variety of artistic pursuits, from oil paintings to bronze sculpture. Born in Arizona and currently residing in California, his love for the West is revealed in his works, which focus on the moods and dignity of the people and their land. Perhaps his inclusion of kaleidoscopes stemmed from a subconscious association with his love of serenity and solitude.

Since earning a Master's Degree in Art at Colorado State in 1956, Tom has been teaching art in the public school system. He initiated a kaleidoscope project for his classes to show his students the infinite possibilities of color and light. His personal interest carried him beyond the experimental cardboard tube variety created in class and ultimately led to the lovely porcelain scopes Tom Proctor now produces.

Despite his attraction to stained glass, Tom wanted to make a different scope from any he had seen. Intrigued by the delicate flesh tones of the porcelain used by his wife Patricia in making dolls, Tom selected three soft pastel shades for the triangular viewing tubes. Then, in marked contrast, he achieved a really unique look by adding sparkling abstract designs on jewel-toned acrylic wheels. The spin of the wheels is as smooth as the glaze on Tom's sleek porcelain scopes.

Kaleidoscopes by
Corki Weeks

Yet another variation of the two-wheel brass and glass kaleidoscope is designed by Corki Weeks. Her asymmetrical placement of multi-textured glass, which includes a neatly angled large gemstone, affords more intricate images than appear in some of the more traditional scopes.

A fiber artist and stained glass craftsman for 15 years, Corki now works full time on kaleidoscopes. Having designed decorative objects for so many years, her thoughts and energies first went into the outside of the scope. Even the cradles to hold the finished product are good-looking and different.

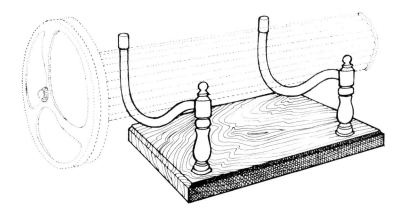

The adventure of looking inside her own scopes and discovering its infinite facets, caused Corki's main point of interest to shift to its interior workings. She also makes a very slim brass scope capped with a faceted crystal. The images in this tube remind me of platinum honeycomb.

Kaleidoscopes by
Dee Potter

It was neither art nor science that attracted Dee Potter to kaleidoscopes. It was an allergy to the sun. Only after moving to Florida did Dee discover that she couldn't enjoy the outdoor life to which she had looked forward. Instead of brooding about it, or moving back north, she decided to refine and expand her hobby of making stained glass pictures.

One experiment led to another and today Dee offers an elegant variation on the two-wheel brass and glass scope. Yes, for the connoisseur and avid collector, Dee will even goldplate the wheels. Front surface mirrors are used in all of these hand-crafted scopes and the wheels are available in stained glass, Brazilian agate or a combination of both. Soon to appear in the shops is a miniature edition of this popular model.

Dee and her husband treat their scopes with great parental care — even in the selection of the shops where they want their craft displayed. Calling on the phone (or visiting in person) periodically, they like to know the people who handle their scopes by name, and most shop owners have become friends.

Through her creation of a mirror-less scope, Dee has single handedly transformed the art of bathing. Since there are no mirrors to fog, the truly addicted can now lounge in the tub while gazing through the tube. This new scope is made from two hollow blown glass cylinders filled with colored oils. This tube within a tube creates a lava-light effect. The wheels are made of fused glass, and as they spin, the oils spiral toward your eye giving a sensation almost like snorkeling in dancing waters with prismatic fish darting to and fro.

Marbelo-Scope
Sue Ross

But enough about wheels for a bit; let's examine a marble scope. Marbles have been around longer than most people realize. Ages ago, they appeared in prehistoric caves and Egyptian tombs. Today they are making a dramatic appearance in kaleidoscopes. In place of an object box or wheels, a marble is fitted onto the end of the scope. By simply moving it around, the view becomes a revolving opalescent mosaic. Marbelo-Scopes are made by Sue Ross.

Featuring fine handmade laticcino marbles, Sue's triangular scopes come in two sizes — one is a neat 7½ inches and the other is an impressive 11 inches. She gives special attention to the soldering aspect of her work, sculpting and beading the copper-finished solder to highlight the merry-go-round iridescent or pastel opaque stained glass exteriors.

A little bag of interchangeable marbles accompanies each scope for an even greater variation of patterns and colors. The finest of optical-coated mirrors provide superb visual images. Sue finds it interesting that while marbles are considered a child's toy, it is the adults who seem to appreciate her Marbelo-Scopes the most.

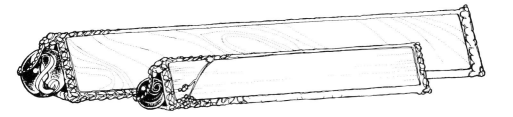

Van Cort Instruments, Ltd.
Erik and Kate Van Cort

Past and present converge enchantingly in the Van Cort scopes. These artful instruments of yesteryear are put together with the modern technology of today's precision tool making. Neither art nor nostalgia, however, was responsible for the beginnings of the Van Cort Kaleidoscopes. Rather, it was a keen sense of business coupled with basic know-how that moved the Van Corts into the scope field.

Erik and Kate had watched with curiosity and amazement as crowds mobbed the kaleidoscope booth at a community crafts fair. When they realized that the kaleidoscope is indeed a scientific yet pleasurable instrument which came into being during the 19th Century, they determined to reproduce a workable model of an original that would be head and shoulders above any others in quality and quantity, at an affordable price.

Erik had been making reproductions of antique scientific instruments such as sun dials, orreries and telescopes for several years and is a collector of optical devices. Kaleidoscopes, quite naturally, became an extension of these interests. The workshop of Van Cort Instruments is housed in a 19th Century New England paper mill. Here they make many models of heirloom quality kaleidoscopes, along with philosophical apparatus of all kinds.

Top of their line is The Classic, an authentic reproduction of Sir David Brewster's original 1820 Parlor Kaleidoscope. It is made of solid brass and mounted on a turned mahogany base. All the optics are precision ground and the chamber box contains handblown glass objects mixed with unusual metal works, thus giving the illusion of Gothic windows. It employs the original design refraction pattern of two top-coated optical mirrors, set at precisely 70 degrees.

Another model, The Monarch, follows the pattern of a late 19th Century kaleidoscope by Charles G. Bush. It is an accurate replica right down to the four-legged base, available in mahogany, ebony or rosewood. This desk model contains many clear crystals along with a few colored glass pieces. When viewed looking into the light, extraordinary crystalline images resembling etched icicles and frosted snowflakes appear. D-Viewing with the light coming from behind, these shimmering illusions take on different hues like the unraveling of a rainbow.

This same crystallized effect can be viewed in the smaller hand-held Woody Kaleidoscopes which are offered in a wide variety of exotic woods. The Lucida, a hand-held solid brass scope and first to bear the Van Cort signature continues to be one of their most popular items along with a tiny clip-on version which is great to have on hand at all times.

Their newest, The Edinburgh, is a parlor scope of contemporary design fitted to a brass and handturned walnut stand. Featuring a massive 3" brass barrel, it is particularly unusual due to its oil/mechanical chamber box. Intricate pieces are specifically designed to be effective in the liquid filled object case.

Companion Kaleidoscope, portable solid brass clip-on (length 5¼")

While Erik busies himself with the scientific intricacies, Kate Van Cort is absorbed with the recipes — those special mixtures of beads and colors and surprises that will insure the same imposing views on the inside as the casings and detailed woodwork provide on the outside.

A winning combination of fastidious attention to detail and superior materials is the hallmark of Van Cort Instruments and is surely responsible for the esteem in which this company is held by the kaleidoscope community.

The Van Corts are "going for the gold" as they put it. Their goals have no boundaries. Having the patronage of the Smithsonian and the Colonial Williamsburg Foundation is a worthy achievement. Now sterling silver scopes are being made for Tiffany Jewelers. Whatever opportunities tomorrow may bring, the Van Corts will be there helping to both create and fulfill each one.

Scepter Scopes
John Culver

John Culver delights in the "kaleidocraze," but doesn't want any part of mass production. Happy and willing to make each part himself, John cleans his mirrors before starting and polishes each completed product. He enjoys and appreciates kaleidoscopes even when they aren't his own. "The mirror is the heart of the scope, and we are the soul," he says, and refers to scopes as "gentle miracles of reflections."

Poetry is another vehicle of his creative mind, a medium which seems to go hand-in-glove with his kaleidoscope production.

"The songs of my soul
give the beat to my heart.
Though I sing them many times,
each time's from the start.

Days of past and future,
Days of present's old,
The things I just remember
Not the things that I've been told.

I shape each day in every way
Within the changing mold
The pleasures of the moments
Just joyously unfold. . . . "

Strongly attracted to marbles, mirrors and magic, John uses them to stunning advantage in "The World Is Your Kaleidoscope." This is the appropriate name of his newest design. Inspired by the achievements of Frank Lloyd Wright, Culver constructed this architectural sculpture which consists of three venetian glass columns, triangular mirrored walls crowned with a spectacular planet marble by Josh Simpson. In some of his smaller models, he uses antique sandwich-glass marbles which are indigenous to his part of New England. "The marble acts as a lens," John explains, "and brings in the fish-eye image of more than 180 degrees. Why, you can even see behind you."

While John is absorbed with light and vision, he is also fascinated by toys, mystical instruments and enchanted objects. In addition to scepter scopes, he makes magic wands and "special moments." John explains his latest artful playthings, "The way to save a moment is to do something with it." "Whether at the hospital while waiting for a friend to come through surgery, during a partial eclipse, or simply waiting for a phone call, use that time to design and make something special." These then are his "moments."

Magic moment   entitled,   I Love You Even
During Eclipses   dated May 30, 1984, 12:48 p.m.

Libraries are an especially important source for Culver's study and research, but his quest for information and knowledge nearly always leads him to people. He listens to their experiences and collects their stories as he travels from place to place around the world. Referring to this pastime as "People's History: Myth and Legend," he related one of his favorite parables about mirrors. . . . "They say if you hold a clear glass in front of yourself, you see the world through it, but if you take that piece of glass and put a thin veneer of silver (money) on it, then all you see is yourself."

"I especially like the way this parable relates to kaleidoscopes. Their magic transcends mirrors that see your image, to mirrors that see inside yourself. This beautiful glimpse both inward and outward, calms and quiets, relaxes and heals! — it awakens the sleeping dreams and calls them forth!"

John shares more than tales and anecdotes. He enjoys teaching friends and family the techniques of making kaleidoscopes, just as he has learned them. In fact, he has shared so many ideas with his sister Ann, she and her husband Pete Roberts are now making a neat little version of their own.

A man of strong faith, John confides, "My creativity doesn't come from me, but through me. I see myself as more of an instrument in the creative process. As it passes through me, I effect it as only I can."

"Little Jack Horner
    sat in a corner
His kaleidoscope to his eye
    He exclaimed with glee
at what he did see
    And looked some more —
with a sigh"

Kaleidoscopia
Tina and Jeff Stasi

The very name sounds like some newly-discovered kingdom where magic is a way of life. Fact is, the wands and scopes created by Tina and Jeff Stasi, proprietors of Kaleidoscopia, look magical.

Jeff refers to scopes as "the toys of infinity," and feels that they "loosen the soul." He also sees them as organizing tools and a consciousness raising device. Making them is, for Jeff, like planting seeds. He believes that, more and more, there is an awareness of the mandala image and its relationship to human consciousness and evaluation.

It was some ten years ago that Jeff, an artist, realized that working with stained glass — windows, boxes and the like — presented a way for him to survive, to travel, to learn and to grow.

Since that time, he has done what he set out to do, and more. He learned from John Culver and Denise Bakke and he worked cooperatively with these people for a few years. Then, each went off in his own direction to do his own thing.

Jeff continued his venture, always reflecting, always perfecting. In 1982, he met Tina who added another welcome dimension to his life, and together they are fulfilling their dream: "creating little windows that look out into an enormous world of light and color."

Kaleidoscopia offers a variety of scopes: stained glass, marble scopes, bamboo marble scopes, bamboo crystal scopes, limited edition dichroic scopes and their extraordinary "magical" wands.

How are wands related to kaleidoscopes? Seen as another outcropping of childhood memories along with costumes, dancing waters, and fairy tales, magic wands are colorful, magical and optical. Jeff and Tina Stasi are making more of these one-of-a-kind glass fantasies as they find more and more wide-eyed interest in them at arts and crafts fairs.

Stained Glass Kaleidoscopes
Charles Karadimos

Charles Karadimos takes as much interest and concern in coordinating the interior colors to harmonize with the exterior casings as he does with the careful selection of stained glass used in all his scopes. With a degree in economics but without formal art background, Charles never considered himself artistic in the "artsy" sense. Others disagreed, however, and soon his tinkerings resulted in terrariums, jewelry boxes, clocks and the like which began selling well at local craft fairs.

It was by "fooling around" with mirrors in some of his glass boxes and making stained glass windows that Charles entered the world of kaleidoscopes. It was just a natural evolution for this self-taught artist. He first exhibited scopes at a show in 1980 and sold all 14 the first day. Trial and error were his teachers and he learned well. He is still learning, he insists. But then he's always enjoyed the experimentation of new ideas and techniques.

Right now he is working with a slumped glass techique which involves heating and fusing flat glass into a bent form. This produces a very smooth and elegant body. To make viewing easy on the eye, the eye piece is actually eye-shaped. Charles completely fills the object boxes with shards and lampworked pieces which enhance the elaborate complexity of the imagery and add a lot of dazzle. He also makes color-coordinated stands and boxes to hold additional object cells.

For a real kaleidophile who needs a scope 'round the clock, Charles does a super custom job. He will photograph the interior of your scope and use the same colors and patterns to design a matching desk or mantle clock.

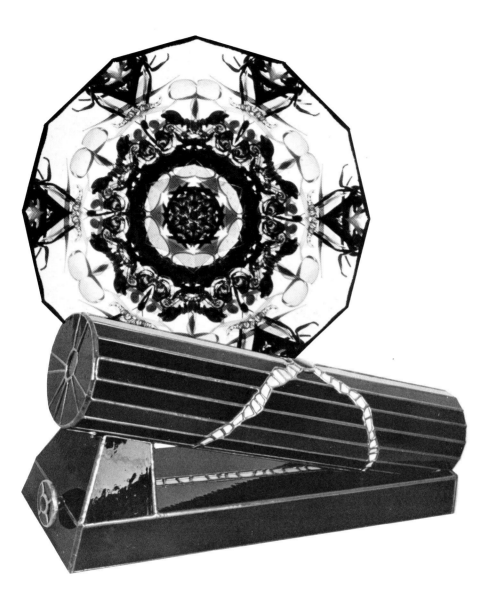

While Charles uses all the colors of the rainbow, he also loves to work with black. Many of his scopes are entirely black, accented with one color, usually white or red. This picture is the prototype of a remarkable table model. Measuring more than 20″ long, its 2-mirror system provides one dramatic image which changes by the turning of a wheel underneath the eyepiece.

Galaxy Glass Works
Annie Greenberg
Craig Huber

Annie Greenberg and Craig Huber have something really new on the drawing board — The Kaleidoscope Game — Transport. They promise it's going to be as exciting as it is colorful. Their future plans also include a variety of optical tools, toys and three-dimensional sculpture.

There wasn't any formal period of research and design for Annie and Craig. In school, Craig was one of those kids who was constantly doodling geometric shapes on his class papers. Clearly, those patterns and ten years of experimenting with stained glass and mirrors provided him with an important base of information.

Dividing the tasks of designing, manufacturing, assembling and shipping, they have transformed their fascination with glass and geometry into a flourishing cottage industry. Annie and Craig feel strongly about the benefits of forming and operating an enterprise where the lines between work and home, business and pleasure have been mostly erased. So their life style is wrapped up in kaleidoscopes — even their neighbors are involved and everyone's happy. "It is a natural blend of our individual passion for geometric symmetry and creative self-expression. We view the kaleidoscope as 'meditation for the eye.'"

Galaxy Glass Works offer a wide variety of scopes in a choice of leather or decorator fabrics. Colors in their oil scopes are brilliant — reminiscent of the way terrestrial bubbles must look.

The Galactiscope is a real eye-teaser with a cascade of dazzling tubular reflections that swirl right up to the eye.

One of their most popular models is the "Create-a-Scope" in

which a removable plastic end cap allows a refill of any objects at all. Left unfilled, it becomes a see-thru scope.

Then there is a nature scope that contains tiny treasures like bits of agate and lacey mosses from their homeland, the Oregon wilderness.

Chromoscopes
David Kalish

David Kalish is a gentleman of many talents. Fascination with illusion led him to the theatre, but an incessant inner tugging drew him back to the visual arts which he has enjoyed from the time he can remember. David finds the kaleidoscope an exciting new canvas upon which to paint.

Chromoscopes are made of acrylic and are truly modern in design. One model, Chromoscope II, combines elements of both the kaleidoscope and teleidoscope. It displays foreground and background simultaneously, providing a three-dimensional effect. The hemispheric lens turns objects of the immediate outside environment into oblong images. The triangular reflecting prism refracts this captured light into a continuously changing pattern of symmetrical forms. Simultaneously, bits and pieces tumble before the prism at random in a constantly changing metamorphosis of brilliant kaleidoscopic visions. The cap at the end is removable so that you can add your own bits of whimsey. Try popping in a few kernels of popped corn — it's wild.

Chromoscope III is a teleidoscope that plays with light in other interesting ways. The black, opaque reflecting prism is bisected by a luminescent magenta or orange window. The free-floating sphere at the end of the prism adds a kinetic effect. Viewed through the eyepiece of the scope, it appears as a suspended liquid bubble, tumbling weightless in space. Light admitted through the luminescent window forms a repetitive series of neon-like triangles surrounding the periphery of the central vision.

David Kalish believes that the most intriguing aspect of the kaleidoscope is its ability to produce, in infinite variation, designs of perfect symmetry. He feels that there is something deep within our nature that universally responds to this impeccable order of symmetry. "In symmetry there is balance; in balance there is harmony; in harmony, equalibrium. As long as we are perfectly balanced, we cannot fall. As long as we do not fall, we continue to survive. Survival is the ultimate and perpetual striving of all living things — from the most primitive to the most sophisticated being. Somewhere therein lies the relationship between the universal appeal of kaleidoscopic mandalas, the inspiration of beauty, the wonder of nature, and the awesome magnificence of Creation itself."

Chromoscopes say it all again and again

Workingwood
Tom and Carol Paretti

Among the wooden kaleidoscopes this one is truly profes-
sionally hewn, smoothly rubbed, and painstakingly polished.
It is hand-crafted by Tom and Carol Paretti at Workingwood.
Out-of-the-ordinary exotic hardwoods like bubinga, zebra-
wood, bocate, koa, African padouk and bird's-eye maple are
buffed until not a seam in the finish nor a grain of the wood
can be felt. Solid velvet! This is a "woodworker's" scope.

The Parettis started making scopes in 1979 because they
felt they couldn't locate any of quality in Arizona. Together
they experimented until they found mirrors and optics to match
the excellence of their fine woodworking; and they now make
several styles.

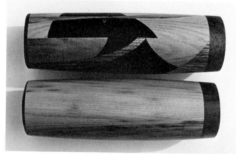

Most popular are their aromatic cedar scopes, possibly because they add a dimension of fragrance. Somehow, the nos-
talgic aroma of grandma's old cedar chest stirs up childhood
recollections in the same way kaleidoscopes do, providing a
double impact.

These cedar scopes are as silky to the touch and fragrant to
the olefactories as they are easy on the eye, resulting in the
viewer's titillating three senses simultaneously.

Top of their lines is an inlaid creation which combines several of the uncommon woods cut into distinctively different
shapes.

Tom and Carol experience pride and joy when crowds are
attracted to their booth at crafts fairs. They are especially
pleased when they learn that teachers are using their scopes
in classrooms, and that doctors purchase them for waiting room
relaxation. But they are really happy when they witness adults'
excitement as they peer through a scope for the first time since
childhood.

Gemscope
Marilyn Endress

This is a gem of a scope. Marilyn Endress recalls the frustration of loving her childhood kaleidoscope but not knowing the secret of its magic, then her despair when she broke open the casing and was left with only the debris of bits of colored glass and plastic beads.

Whether it was this early experience or the innate creative talents which developed as she matured, Marilyn produces Gemscopes that are beautiful and well made. Her business is aptly named because she uses gems like amethysts crystals, Brazilian and moss agates, carnelian garnets, rose quartz, peridot and faceted Austrian crystals. Optic quality mirrors capture crisp, distortion-free images and a thin oil in the chamber allows the colors to dance with more alacrity than is usual in oil-suspension scopes.

Seashells and swirly glass marbles enhance the finely detailed designs, and the bits and pieces seem to be blown about by colored winds. The smart brass tube is just different enough in size to be really comfortable to hold, and fits into one of the neatest felt-lined stands around. This and the recessed eyepiece are made of Honduran mahogany. The lacquered scope is capped with a leaded crystal to add even more dazzle.

Looking at the flowery floating images in a gemscope is like looking at a picture post-card of heaven's gardens.

Marilyn has some big plans for the future including some very large scopes that have an internal light source and sophisticated mechanisms. The creative flow has been touched off. Marilyn says, "creativity has to come from within, you know, before it can be manifested in the outer realm."

For Your Eyes
Joe Kerby

Joe Kerby, a Missouri dentist who makes "For Your Eyes" kaleidoscopes, humorously notes that he couldn't very well call his scope business "For Your Teeth." Yet, you might well get the impression that this unique product, with all its extra lenses and discs, could be the work of an optometrist.

Each Kerby kaleidoscope comes with three insertable lenses and two interchangeable discs, a brass stand and the optical tube. The Kerby tube truly incorporates the fine art of stained glass and the delicate mastery of laser (front surface) mirror. Each tube is made up of 155 individually cut, wrapped and soldered pieces of art glass. The mirror embedded within the tube can be made to take the shape of either a triangular or square configuration.

"I believe I'm one of the only artists to produce a square-mirrored kaleidoscope in the country . . . its development came primarily because of the shape of the tiny squares which individually comprise the tube," Joe says.

Even though Kerby is somewhat new to the scope scene, he has stamped some neoteric notions of his own onto his work. The insertable lens occurred to him one day when he placed the tube in front of the venetian blinds, a practice he still enjoys. He thought, "If only a design could be stationary while the disc turns, that would be something!" Indeed, it is — like adding streaks of brushed lightening.

Joe and his wife Mary find endless pleasure in looking through the kaleidoscope while listening to music. "Cloudy days are best," he confides. "Each turn of the disc brings a new brilliant color display. That, along with the relaxing music provides us with a renewed knowledge of our Heavenly origin," says Joe, quoting an appropriate scripture:

"I have heard of thee by the hearing of the ear; but now mine eye seeth thee."

— Job 42:5

Prism Designs
Tim Grannis
Jack Lazarowski

Sleekly modern, yet graceful in design, the glass sparkles and the metal shines. Tim Grannis is first of all a sculptor, then a jeweler. "My concerns are with 3-dimensionality, the fluidity of form and line and the dance of light over reflective surfaces."

Jack Lazarowski worked as an industrial and graphic designer before he started building gold and silver flutes and piccolos. From there he, too, moved into jewelry. Tim and Jack have combined their talents and energies. Together they are making jewel-like music in the form of a participatory sculptural kaleidoscope.

Some of their scopes have prismatic arrangements of mirrors and transparent glass within prisms, within other prisms, that multiply fractions of images — no wonder their trade name is Prism Designs! Multiple colors and patterns repeating themselves in the mirrors of themselves.

Another style uses beveled glass panels in place of mirrors, so that an image coming through the end of the scope is broken up into kaleidoscopic patterns — then overlapping — they are the images that come through the transparent sides of the instrument which are refracted and overlapped again so that there is a double imaging of the environment.

Tim and Jack think that the scope should be handsome, not merely a cylinder that comes alive only when you look through it. It is a light machine that sits on the table 24 hours a day as an ornament. They also find the exposed inner workings optically exciting. So they have taken the scope out of its tube, showing just how it is made — the workings of the lenses and mirrors. They are right — it is beautiful and visually stimulating. They put it this way: "We like seeing the kaleidoscope as a way of encouraging people to look at their environment in a slightly different way."

Colorscopes by Kosage
Ken and Cheryl Kosage

"Beauty is in the Eye of the Holder" — that is the clever line of Colorscopes by Kosage. *Love of their Colorado outdoors and a fascination with the effects of light prisms moved Ken and Cheryl into the scope field and has kept them there. Although the Kosages are now represented in galleries throughout the country, it is still the one-to-one association with the customers on the craft show circuit that they enjoy.*

In their desire to capture various forms of prismatic images, they first created the traditional type stained glass scopes. Then, doing what came naturally to them, they developed a scope using dried wild flowers which provides the viewer with the illusion of being drawn inside a flower garden. This brings to mind a reference made in a French magazine shortly after Brewster invented the Scope. It said, in part, that the Chinese who were familiar with this wonderful instrument called it a wan-boa-Tang, which means "tube of a thousand flowers."

The Kosages have designed their own ceramic tube. This is one of the very few ceramic scopes around, and they use it to accommodate their entire line, which includes dried flowers, stained glass or Austrian gazing-ball crystals. Each smoothly glazed ceramic cylinder is decorated with a flower design. A hand-oiled select wood stand cradles each scope.

The Kosages have a deep respect for tradition, and they are hoping customers will come to think of their scope as an heirloom to be passed down.

"We live in a world that is so 'on the go,' that if we can lend a small part in exposing people to a time gone by when people were more content with simple beauties, then we will feel a continued growth from our art."

Kaleidoscopes by
Rick Palosky

Rick Palosky admires the great masters of the arts and strives to be counted among them as a creator of fine kaleidoscopes. Already a master goldsmith, silversmith and stained-glass craftsman, Rick says the scopes are "a natural evolution, plus my own design inclinations." From the moment he became inspired to utilize his talents for the creation of a kaleidoscope, he knew that he wanted it to look like something that Michaelangelo, DaVinci or Faberge had created for his own personal use.

Rick's inspiration was more than a dream. He knew he had to produce a work of art, using only the finest, the most beautiful materials; and, indeed, the products he markets are representative of his personal desires.

Whether the housing is brass, marble, silver or gold, the material is genuine and solid. The Palosky scope is driven by gears which enable the viewer to change and control the view with the most absolute precision. Completely handmade these one-of-a-kind, Belle-Epogue style scopes have a "quietly crude" quality which gives them a resemblance to models of old.

From simple dried flowers like forget-me-nots and Queen Ann's Lace to precious gems like emeralds, diamonds, rubies and opals, Rick is attempting to embody both the quality of nature and the dazzle of precious gems into the scopes he produces. His ambition is to make the most beautifully bejeweled kaleidoscope in the world — the Faberge of kaleidoscopes!

Victorian Visions
Robert & Stella Morehead

The name of the Morehead's mail order toy business is Americana Nostalgia. It was only natural when they decided to integrate the concept of toy with art, in the form of a kaleidoscope, that they call it Victorian Visions. It also has a sub-title, "Ephemeral Images of Exquisite Beauty" and a sub-sub-title,"Gothic Cathedral" stained glass kaleidoscopes. Their scopes are all of those — and more.

The Victorian Visions "gothic" model brings the rich tapestry of a cathedral window into the interior of a kaleidoscope. As the round "windows" are rotated on their axis, their intense colors and complex patterns appear to extend far beyond the confines of the kaleidoscope's interior. Each wheel contains thirteen different pieces of glass. Each of the twenty six pieces is chosen as much for its varying textures as for its color and transparency.

Each piece of stained glass is first cut into shape and its edges are carefully ground so that a perfect circle is formed absolutely without gaps between the various pieces. Each piece of glass is then wrapped with copper foil and soldered together. The seams are "beaded" by flowing on molten solder, which results in a strong permanent seam. This was the method used by Tiffany and his contemporaries in making lamps and other figural pieces. When soldering is completed, the seams, feet and eyepiece of the mirror tube are then sculpted and polished with files. The smooth polished metal is pleasant to the touch; and its sleek, straight lines enhance the total streamlined appearance of the kaleidoscope.

The optical quality mirrors in this kaleidoscope are the same as those found in telescopes and scientific instruments. This provides bright distortion-free images.

In discussing the merits of the two-mirror system vs. the three-mirror, Robert made an interesting observation: "A consideration of the metaphysical implications of the equilateral kaleidoscope provides another possible explanation of its powerful attraction. As the triangular pattern of the mirrors move toward the periphery of the field of view, they appear to recede into infinity in geometrical orderly fashion. This implies a framework or grid which 'controls' the random complex images reflected in them. Is the kaleidoscope thus a subconscious analogy of the 'clockwork' universe which man finds so much more comforting than that of a universe of chaos in which all apparent 'order' is due to man's own limited perceptions? Perhaps the kaleidoscope is a truly magical device which allows our sense of sight a glimpse of that which can only be perceived within the abstract confines of our minds."

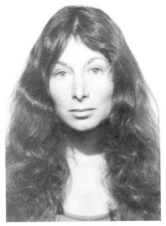

Fantasy Glass
Lesley Wadsworth

This lady's scopes are really quite different. "Fantasy Glass by Lesley" is coated with up to twenty different layers of metal oxide. Certain wave lengths of light will pass through and others will be reflected. The light rays which don't get through the coated glass appear to take on the color characteristics of the metal formula. The reason the glass changes color when viewed from different angles has to do with Laws of Refraction and a difference in the Refractive Index between air, glass and the metal layers.

The results are worth seeing, even if the description tends to boggle the mind. A few of her scopes use this same type of laser glass for the eyepiece, which means that the wheels are reflected on to the eyepiece and then reflected back on to the wheel, giving even more depth to the colors. This is one of the few scopes that is even more astonishing when viewed with artificial light than with sunlight.

Based in the San Francisco Bay area, Lesley Wadsworth has obviously given a great deal of time and thought to creating a scope that is most unusual. Interiors and exteriors receive the same oxidized treatment and this method results in colors not usually found in the normal range. Each scope is covered in suedecloth, with cut-outs along the sides to admit even more sparkle.

The sights and sounds of childhood, like penny candy, fireflys and fireworks are captured in these thin wheels of visual magic.

"Blessed are the eyes which see what you see!"
— Luke 10:23

88

Spirit Scopes
Willie and Alice Stevenson

Something big and special is being built at Spirit Scopes — a 5½ foot floor model. A flame oxidized copper barrel three inches in diameter and sixteen inches long is mounted on a hand forged wrought iron stand. The eye piece and object case are made of hand-turned rosewood. For comfortable viewing, the scope is attached to an adjustable swivel mount that rotates 360° and tilts to adjust for height. A small crank near the eyepiece turns to change the patterns in a choice of four interchangeable object cases (one is left empty to fill with your own jewels). An identical table model is available.

Kaleidoscope making for Willie and Alice Stevenson was an accidental, but very natural combination of their blacksmithing and glassworking skills. They live in a small mountain town in North Carolina, that time has by-passed. The Stevensons have given up the traditional life style to pursue art and learn deeper lessons in the "walk of faith." In honor of the Guiding Light they have named their enterprise "Spirit Scopes."

"Our first 'fancy' scope was rather awkward, in retrospect," Alice admits. "But we thought it was wonderful and we called the dim optics 'ethereal' instead of fuzzy, which they were!" Today they use high percentage, first surface mirrors.

In developing fluid-filled object cases, they experimented with everything available, including Karo syrup. Now they use a "magic fluid" in which they float stained glass flakes and threads, semi-precious stones, wire forms and found objects. Each scope is meticulously hand built of copper and no two are alike. The end result is a striking piece of flame oxidized sculpture which dazzles the eye and soothes the spirit. Petal type prongs are flanged so that it sits upright on its built-in base.

Après la Pluie
(After the Rain)
Dominique Stora

Dominique Stora brings his vast inventory to America from France.

Dominique started making kaleidoscopes in Paris in 1976, before he was aware of the scope boom in America. He remembers that his mother loved kaleidoscopes and gave many to him during his youth. When he and his wife opened a shop of old books and toys they were constantly on the look-out for some antique kaleidoscopes. Nearly all they found were in bad condition so Dominique decided to make some himself.

Aided and abetted by some knowledge of optics which stemmed from his interest in photography, Dominique started making and selling them in his shop. He says his only regret is that so much time is spent in the production, bookkeeping and postal chores there is little time left for new creations. However, he has already designed more than 20 models which he distributes in more than 20 countries.

One metal scope which attracts a lot of attention has a holographic eye positioned at the end of the tube, which produces a rather startling effect. The interior view is almost as big a surprise because the mirrors being square, create very different and unexpected patterns. Some of Dominique's tubes are covered with leather, others with a decorative marbelized paper and still others are made of metal.

Small wooden pieces, resembling chess figures are collectors' items. Some are inlaid with mother-of-pearl and others with ivory and turquoise. There is also a tiny hand-painted china scope and one that can be worn as a necklace available in brass or black aluminum. You name it, Apres la Pluie makes it.

Dominique's ambition is to enlarge his range of creativity and to become a specialist in these "poetic objects which by their effective simplicity of design stimulate the imagination and induce dreams."

A Touch of Glass
Gary Newlin
Howard Roe

Whether tucked between hot dog stands at a country fair or set up along the parade route that leads to a community oyster roast, the Touch of Glass booth is a major attraction. The interest of the crowds that gather is infectious. "I haven't seen one of these since I was a kid," and "How I used to love these," are common exclamations as people stop to admire Gary Newlin's display.

His shop in Asheville, North Carolina, is also quite a sight, chockfull of colored glass in every shape and form. Along with articles left for repair, you will find kaleidoscopes in abundance. Some scopes are finished and rest in wooden cradles, but most of them are packaged in kits that bear instructions easy enough for an eight-year-old to follow and complete in less than an hour.

It is these inexpensive kits that serve a purpose very close to the heart of Gary Newlin. Materials include a copper tube, two copper caps, three mirrors, cardboard, chips of glass, styrofoam, masking tape and glue. These components don't sound very impressive, but assembling them and seeing the finished product bring a great deal of joy to whoever does it . . . particularly to the exceptional children on whom Gary Newlin has been concentrating for some time.

Before opening A Touch of Glass, Gary's career was in childhood development, so it was natural to blend his interests and his talents. The results are very rewarding.

Mentally and physically handicapped children are not often accorded a leisure-time activity other than television. "Most of them have never been allowed to do anything like this before," he explains. "When they start seeing the colors and making the kaleidoscopes, they get fired up."

But, the real satisfaction comes when the children finish their work. "They get positive feedback," Gary says with enthusiasm. "And that makes them feel good. It gives them increased feelings of worth."

The World's Largest Kaleidoscope
Alfred Brickel

The Guinness Book of World Records does not have a category — yet — for kaleidoscopes, but Alfred Brickel did receive a letter from Guinness Superlatives Ltd., stating that his was the largest on record.

The kaleidoscope weighs 500 lbs., is 123" overall and 75" high. The object box is 48" in diameter and the viewing image is 36". The box is 23" × 10½" × 77" and it is operated with gears and pulleys.

Al Brickel is a partner of Newe Daisterre Glas (Morning Star Glass, Middle English), an art glass studio which does hand-crafted custom work. The "world's largest kaleidoscope" was made-to-order for a bar of that name in Cleveland, which never opened. Al is happy that the scope not only survived, but is appreciated even more today.

Its operation is totally different since the 4' object box, which he refers to as a "squirrel cage" rotates on a horizontal plane. It is made for comfortable viewing while standing and the image changes by the turning of two ship's wheels. Almost any type objects can be easily inserted, providing multiple effects — a kaleidoscopic carrousel of colors and forms.

Kaleidoplex
Marshall Yeager
Walter Reike

A person steps into his own world of vision in a kaleidoscope. The experience is personal. Only the viewer is seeing and feeling this mystical phenomenon. Part of the charm and intrigue is in this very privacy. It's almost as though it holds magic secrets for the viewer alone.

I was afraid projecting the images on a screen and sharing the experience with others would diminish the impact of "splendid isolation." So it was with trepidation that I viewed the Kaleidoplex. My fears were unfounded. The experience was uplifting, exhilerating, eye-boggling — in fact, I could exhaust all my magnificent superlatives and still be at a loss for words!

Synchronized dancing patterns come and go, and go to come again. "It's all done with mirrors," says the kaleidoplex inventor Marshall Yeager. "The light projection device is based on the principle of the kaleidoscope," he explains. Quite simply, the Kaleidoplex creates colored imagery to sound.

The prototype project, built from Yeager's designs, was developed by Walter Reike of East Coast Camera Center, Inc. Reike's machine is an impressive red and black collection of mirrors, lenses, motors, and aluminum almost three feet long, 14 inches high, and weighing 65 pounds. He is now building a small version of this machine for home viewing.

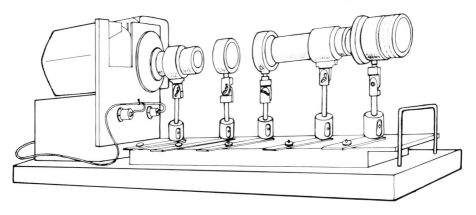

Marshall became interested in the kinetic art form of lights while he was a co-producer of the sound and light spectacular, "Heavy Organ" starring Virgil Fox, which premiered in New York City in the 70's and toured for many years.

As a result of this involvement, Marshall did research and experimented until he discovered an optical principle that allowed him to send a projected kaleidoscopic image into a second kaleidoscope projecting apparatus. This method was the basis for Yeager's patent. It is the same technique which will be reduced into a workable size for everyone to enjoy.

To watch the mesmerizing mandalic images projected by a kaleidoplex while listening to music will provide the ultimate kaleidoscopic experience in the confines of one's own home — the embodiment of an ultra imaginative vision.

So the scope world that began with the Scottish gentleman, Sir David Brewster, endures and expands.

Even as this book goes to press, I am sure there are new kaleidoscopes being developed. Of yet unborn scopes, Brewster said, "to what degree of perfection it may yet arrive at, is not easy to anticipate." Today this is still true, for who knows what thrilling colors and unexpected patterns are yet to be viewed in scopes of the future?

Section III

Related Facets and Inner Reflections

Kaleidoscope
The kaleidoscope speaks silently
Whispering secrets to man's inner-space
Colors infuse the psyche with joy
As synchronized patterns spin into place.

Related Facets and Inner Reflections

Eighteen books have been published with the word "kaleido-scope" in the title, but not one of these books deals with the subject of kaleidoscopes. The word "kaleidoscope" has become synonymous with anything involving rapid change, variation of colors and patterns, or even the thrill of the unexpected.

For the scope maker, kaleidoscope is another word for feel-ing. It is a bridge between him, his fellow man and the Supreme Creative Artist. One collector says to be alone with a kaleido-scope is like being with a good friend whose company you want to last forever.

Bringing together in one object cell a unity of light, color, form and motion that seems to capture moments of eternity, the kaleidoscope "inspires the mind" and "calls the heart." It is the only art form which is continuously and endlessly being created right before the viewer's eyes. The static has been removed and the imagery lives, equating itself to life's experiences.

"The world is your kaleidoscope,
and the varying combinations of colors
which it presents to you at every succeeding
moment are the exquisitely adjusted images
of your ever moving thoughts."

James Allen

"The World is your Kaleidoscope" by John Culver

Bennett Synphonoscope

Peach Reynolds

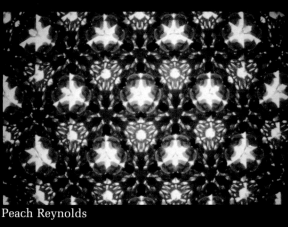

Peach Reynolds

Kaleidoplex

Doug Johnson

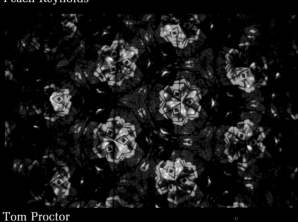

Tom Proctor

GalloColley Glass

COSMIC
Woman

AN ORIGINAL KLÄJESCOPE™
(COLLAGE · A · SCOPE)

BY CARMEN AND STEPHEN COLLEY
USING OPTICAL QUALITY MIRROR
AND BALL BEARING MOVEMENT

ALSO:
49 AUSTRIAN LEAD CRYSTALS AND BEADS
15 FACETED GLASS JEWELS AND BEADS
CULTURED PEARL
OPALS
ADVENTURINE LEAF
AMETHYST
GARNET
CITRINE
AQUAMARINE
SYNTHETIC ALEXANDRITE, EMERALD, AND
SAPPHIRE

BRAZILIAN AGATE
ROSE QUARTZ

FUSED GLASS BY CARMEN AND STASHE
SANDBLASTED DESIGNS, BLOWN GLASS,
AND CARD BY STEPHEN

ANTIQUE BUTTON
RETICELLI ROD
CZECHOSLOVAKIAN SEED BEADS
ANCIENT GLASS FROM ISRAEL
GLASS MARBLES FOR FEET
SHIBORI BAG BY MARQUETTA JOHNSON
GLASSES: ANTIQUE CATHEDRAL, FLUTED,
AND IRRIDESCENT

ANTIQUE COPPER FINISH

THIS KALEIDOSCOPE IS UNIQUE
AND THE DESIGN WILL NOT BE
REPEATED.

99

Northampton Studios

Once toys — now antiques

Colorscopes by Kosage

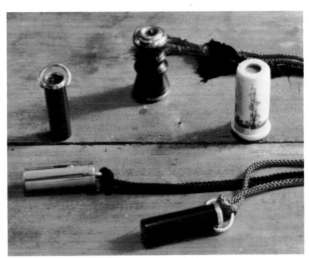

Ray Howlett   Après la Pluie

Après la Pluie

Prism Designs

Gemscope

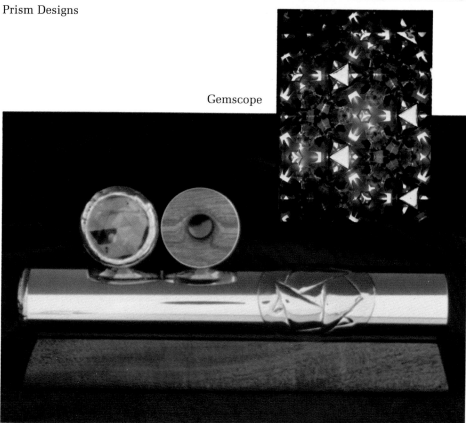

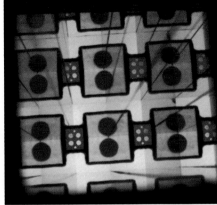

For Your Eyes

Galaxy Glass

Victorian Visions

Laughing Coyote

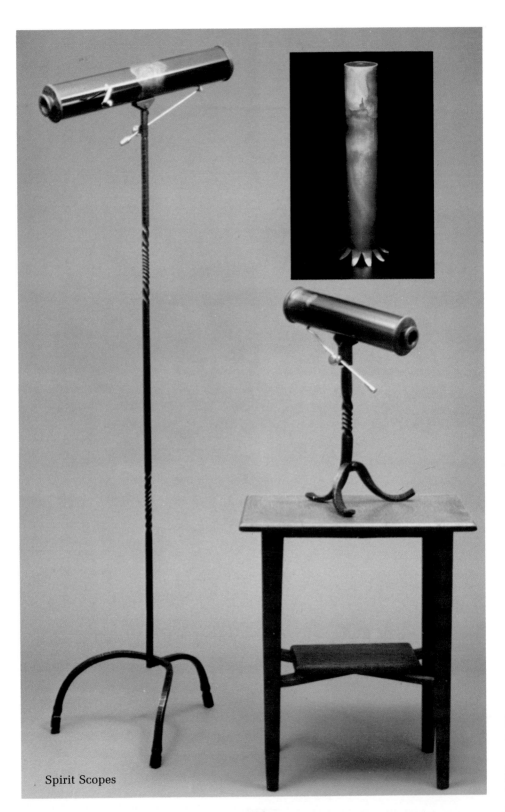

Spirit Scopes

106

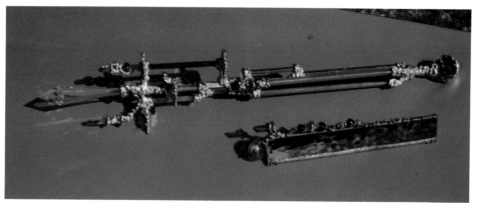

Magic wand and scope by Kaleidoscopia

Stained Glass Kaleidoscopes
by Karadimos

Van Cort Instruments, Ltd.

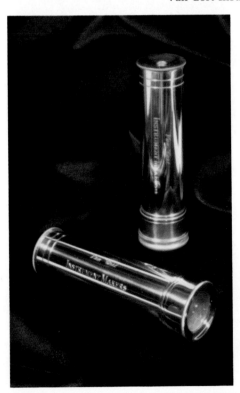

Colorscopes by Irene Holler

Kaleidostitch by Mary Ann Saber

A Kenneth Kaufman photograph of kaleidoscopic effects in nature.

Quilt by Mary Golden

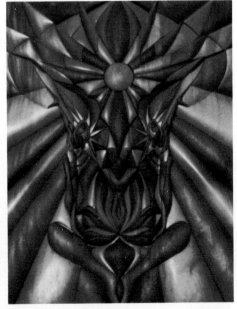

Wooden puzzle-sculpture
by Brian Tompkins

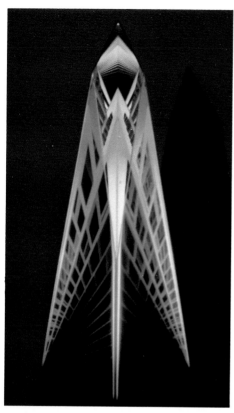

Ray Howlett   Inner-light sculpture   Robert Stephan

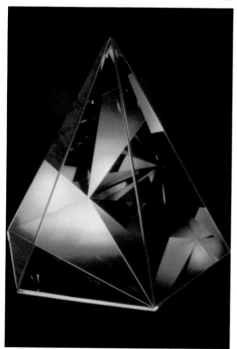

The author photographed through Bennett scopelens™
Floral abstractions photographed in nature by Judith Karalitz©

Mandala

The word "mandala" appears in this book almost as many times as the word kaleidoscope. It may be appropriate to examine this term and discover why it comes to mind with each facet of the kaleidoscope.

A mandala is a circle expanding from its individual center as it interrelates with other circles, spiraling forth from their center, all being one with the creative universal source. It is a circle whose center is everywhere and whose bounds are non-existent.

There are three basics inherent in both the kaleidoscope and the mandala: a center, cardinal points and symmetry. In a mandala, as in the patterns of a kaleidoscope, a succession of interlinkings are unified into one whole. Each piece is a vital part of that whole, no matter how small. Take one piece away and the image is not quite the same.

Beyond its inherent beauty and captivating magic, the kaleidoscope symbolizes life — a mandala in action. Man is the center. The awakening of intelligence is the first radiating circle, spiraling from the center and proceeding from there, each person's mandala is as individual and distinctively different as a fingerprint.

The unfolding drama of human events and emotions tumbles and spills from an inexhaustible source on no apparent course. But the universe is fashioned and governed according to a principal of divine order. We sense it, we know it's there, but the breadth and complexity of its patterns make it invisible to our mind's eye.

Only man's awareness and attunement to the Creative Original Force determine whether the patterns in his mandala fall at random or seek a meaningful direction. The archetype referred to by Carl Jung, represents a pattern of order in which each content falls into proper place and the tumbling pieces are held together by a protective circle — the microcosmic enclosed within the macrocosmic.

The way we see and view the conditions in our life is the way our personal mandala unfolds. Circumstances are prototypes which we understand, or misunderstand, in accordance with our level of consciousness. Situations occur in order that we become centered; growing and developing as our individuality evolves — a mandala — a palette of life's experiences.

Color

Ancient man revered the supernatural aspect of color, finding in it the symbols for everything in life and death. A study of color through the ages reveals that at any given period in history colors played a significant role with respect to superstitions, religions, philosophies, traditions and even the daily activities of people.

It is said that only in more recent times did the aesthetic and sensuous pleasures of color come into play, and it was then that color was relegated to a more or less taken-for-granted status. Fortunately there is a serious reappraisal of the significance and influence of color underway. Color is in! There are books on color harmony, color psychology, color therapy, color healing and even books on how to color youself beautiful.

The significance of the prismatic spectrum is found in everything in life — from angels to zoetrobes. All creation is a technicolor panorama projected on life's screen of space. And each element of the universe vibrates to its own corresponding color, as everything in the world works in harmony with the chromatic color scale.

The seven colors of the spectrum are attuned to the seven tones of the musical scale. And as each color runs the gamut of shades, it has its own corresponding note on a higher or lower octave. The three primary colors comprise the first major scale.

Every zodiac sign has a particular color transmitted to earth by means of the sun. Each planet in our solar system receives one of the seven rays of color. There is even a philosophy of color in relation to minerals and precious stones, and flowers. Each emotion and organ of the body possesses its own particular color and responds to it in a specific way.

The therapeutic and healing value of colors, and how they affect our emotional, mental and spiritual body are well recognized. Color is energy. By experimenting with color and gazing into a kaleidoscope, the proper vibration alignment may be activated in mind and body. Red represents the material realm while violet, at the other end of the spectrum, is the spiritual sphere. Green is the balancing stabilizer between the three stimulating colors (red, orange and yellow) and the three calming colors (blue, indigo and violet).

But while the properties of color may be universal, the true perception of color remains personal and individual, with each person possessing his own spectral aura.

Efrocine, a dress designer, colorist and textile painter, equates the body to a human kaleidoscope. She believes the sacred attar of the heart is the center of light, the focal point of the flow of life in each individual. In a "living color" workshop, she cites the theory of the 16th Century Italian painter, Paolo Veronese, who earned his title, "Magician of Light." He saw beauty as the most powerful catalyst for enlightenment. In his quest for beauty, he ignored the dull browns and grays of his predecessors and painted in full light, making his graceful figure iridescent, nearly transparent. Veronese was the first to capture on canvas the sweeping movement of an angel in flight.

Efrocine teaches that "by finding colors which harmonize with our body-soul light, our aura is activated. We become living color. An inner radiance permeates our whole being, so that we are transformed, and transported into a realm of exquisite beauty. By surrounding ourselves in our living color, we accept into our being 'a Benediction of Light'."

The full spectrum of color has never been perceived as brilliantly as seen through the inner eye of a blind woman.

> I understand how scarlet can differ from crimson because I know that the smell of an orange is not the smell of a grapefruit. I can also conceive that colors have shades and guess what shades are. In smell and taste there are varieties not broad enough to be fundamental; so I call them shades . . . The force of association drives me to say that white is exalted and pure, green is exuberant, red suggests love or shame or strength. Without the color or its equivalent, life to me would be dark, barren, a vast blackness.

> Thus through an inner law of completeness my thoughts are not permitted to remain colorless. It strains my mind to separate color and sound from objects. Since my education began I have always had things described to me with their colors and sounds, by one with keen senses and a fine feeling for the significant. Therefore, I habitually think of things as colored and resonant. Habit accounts for part. The soul sense accounts for another part. The brain with its five-sensed construction asserts its right and accounts for the rest. Inclusive of all, the unity of the world demands that color be kept in it whether I have cognizance of it or not. Rather than be shut out, I take part in it by discussing it, happy in the happiness of those near to me who gaze at the lovely hues of the sunset or the rainbow.

> — Helen Keller

Kenneth Kaufman

The multi-faceted mural of the world is a kaleidoscope. "Peering into the world of nature is much like peering into the world of kaleidoscopes," says Kenneth Kaufman in a book to be published soon. Color and design explode in unison from Kenneth's photographic portrayals of his kaleidoscopic perspectives. He uses the great outdoors as the object case for his camera. Kenneth explores visually the various kaleidoscopic effects and elements observed in nature: light, symmetry, form, movement, collage, color:

— "As light gives life, it also creates possibilities for the most memorable visual experience. It is the effect of light that gives nature her special kaleidoscopic appearance and personality . . .

— "Nature regularly reveals aspects of herself in a measured, symmetrical fashion. And the presence of symmetry gives a particular scene in nature, overall balance . . . or equity and evenness. Foliage dangling from the trees. Reeds protruding from the woods . . . hills reflecting on the ponds . . . mirrored clouds upon a lake . . . in each instance, the possibility of a naturally-occurring symmetrical relationship is there, readily observable to the perceptive eye . . .

— Very little stagnates, nor remains the same in nature either. There is a constant renewal, rebirth . . .

— The kaleidoscope of patterns to be discovered in nature . . . makes one wonder — How did such order and sense come about? This question is still asked . . . the answer to it remains a wonderful mystery."

Irene Holler

Irene Holler is a believer in divine order, whether it be in the universe or artistic designs. Painting objects and scenes in repeated segments which radiate from the center, Irene translates kaleidoscopic pictures onto canvas. She calls them "colorscopes."

As a child, Irene was frustrated by the fact that a treasured view in a kaleidoscope would vanish with just a tiny movement of the wrist, never to return. She found a way to have her view and keep it too. Using watercolors, ink, colored pencils, acrylics or egg tempura as well as oils, Irene converts figures and fantasies, by way of pigments and brush, into emotionally charged mandalas.

The works themselves draw the viewer into the heart of the picture and lead the eye around the painting from image to repeated image through the use of carefully thought-out designs. Even though the colorscopes are inspired by the abstract patterns and colors of the kaleidoscope, they retain a recognizable subject matter. For example, they may take the form of Kushan water urns, Iowa tribe moccasins, carnival figures, quilt patterns, or unicorns and castles. They all radiate in multiple repeating segments. Each part of the painting is a mirror image of itself in exacting detail, yet the viewer never tires of looking and "seeing" more.

Joyously enthusiastic about her own creations, Irene says, "In my colorscopic designs, I have not consciously devised a way to lift one into other realms of consciousness; however, personal thoughts and feelings of the viewer do so."

Irene believes along with Carl Jung that patterns produced by mandalas "touch the unconscious, calling forth arch types that transcend civilization and cultures."

Ray Howlett   Robert Stephan

Two artists who employ inner light in their treatment of glass acknowledge that many people remark on the kaleidoscopic appearance of their work.

An optical technician in space light sculpture, Ray Howlett's ideas encompass a precise, skillful combination of etched and dichroic-coated glass shapes that are lighted from within. The light images are repeatedly reflected inward and turn into a vast array of color. There seems to be space where there is no space.

Ray is experimenting with sculptures that are really transparent kaleidoscopes — a total environment scope. As a person looks inside, everything in the room is visible, viewed at a distance, it is all color, because the sides and ends are transparent and yet highly reflective.

It is a viewer participation art form that to some may inspire meditation.

Robert Stephan is endeavoring to bring a fresh new style of design into the glass medium by using internal colors and air inclusions in his designs. "The real challenge," Robert says, "is to successfully combine the varying factors of blown glass, transparency, light and color all into one finished piece."

He taught himself the fundamentals of hot glass and fabricated his first furnace from a fifty-five gallon steel drum. "My fascination with this unique medium involves manipulating a hot fluid mass into a finished glassform as it cools and becomes a solid."

118

In one of his pieces the form and colors resemble dancing fountains. Each sculpture is a statement of the artist's "joy in creation and the beauty inherent in God's world."

Mary Golden

Mary Golden, a quilter and teacher of quilting in New England is writing a book on Kaleidoscope Quilts. "My approach to designing a kaleidoscope quilt is similar to that of a painter," she explains. "Fabric pieces are placed upon a fabric base one at a time like dabs of oil paint upon a canvas or as the chips of glass fall in the object box of a kaleidoscope. Patterns begin to develop and subtle secondary patterns emerge later to create layers and depth. I feel that the quilt is successful when it can be viewed in every light, in every setting and with every mood and the designs appear to be ever-changing."

Mary uses an old design to demonstrate her ability to "see beyond the block." In this old pattern, a careful arrangement of simple triangles, large and small, can fool the eye into seeing large circles despite the fact that a kaleidoscope quilt has no curved lines.

The basic unit of a kaleidoscope quilt is a square block divided into eight equal quadrants, radiating from a central axis. "It is this radiant division of the space that has attracted me to the kaleidoscope pattern," Mary says, "and more than that, beyond quilt making to encompass all of nature. For I suspect that much of the harmony that exists in the cosmos originates from these evergrowing circles — like a mandala."

119

Brian Tompkins

Even wooden sculpture takes on kaleidoscopic overtones in Brian Tompkin's wooden puzzles. Brian discovered Chesshire's Mandala kaleidoscope while pursuing visual art studies at Dartmouth. He was so intrigued that he took one with him on a hitchhiking trek across the country.

He enjoyed sharing it with the good-hearted people who would pick him up and on a few occasions he introduced it to shop keepers along the way, thus becoming a self-motivated kaleidoscope salesman.

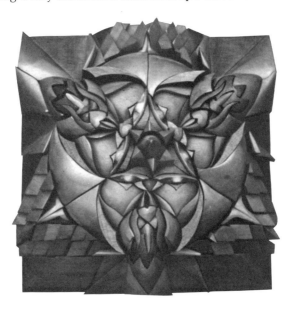

Brian managed to attend quite a few "Grateful Dead" concerts during that summer, and at one point, used the kaleidoscope to design a Grateful Dead Mandala. A senior project turned his first Mandala into a 4' x 4' version. From this, his puzzle-sculpture evolved.

His early works confronted one with cartoony humor and geometry. Then he progressed to themes with more symbolism and spirituality.

Mandalic, centered, but centerless, Brian's well-formed puzzles offer viewers many meditational levels — the grain of the wood, the finely turned glow of three finishes and the triple dimensions of the graphic. Brian strives "to pull all the light of the wood to the surface — to let the wood's spirit shine."

Mary Ann Saber

Mary Ann Saber sews a very fine seam indeed, with gold and silver metallic thread. While Mary Ann believes the old proverb, "a stitch in time saves nine," she is convinced that the same stitch is nine times more beautiful when replicated kaleidoscopically.

After looking at some exotic Chinese silk through a teleidoscope, Mary Ann was inspired to switch her oriental embroidery design to geodesic and mandalic patterns. Creating a new concept and coining a new term "kaleidostitch," Mary Ann interprets fine embroidery in one-of-a-kind hand-stitched paintings on silk.

She makes her own embroidery floss from silk and metallic threads; and while the delicate stitching looks complicated, actually only one simple stitch is employed — couching. This is a method of laying a long heavier thread on top of the work and securing it in place with small overlapping stitches of a finer thread.

Mary Ann combines, in one design, form and color that seem to move — providing yet another inventive facet to the Kaleidorama.

Helmut and Charlene Goral

Another craft bearing the mandala signature is Mandala Candles. Helmut and Charlene Goral have been making candles for 14 years. Geometric patterns were hard to perfect, but they hit on something that pleased them and seems to please the customers at crafts fairs.

They asked friends to help come up with a catchy name for their mathematical candles, and went straight to the dictionary when someone suggested Mandala. The definition fit precisely.

Mandala candles are made by folding layers of different colored wax into a pattern. Cross sections are taken from the pattern and are then applied symmetrically to a clear core of wax. Each candle is shaped by hand.

When lit, the light glows through the pattern, turning it into a small stained wax window. Most people think they are too pretty to light. But after burning for two to four hours until there is an even hole down the center, the candle may be refilled with a votive candle — turning it into an eternal mandala.

Ned Herrmann, artist, sculptor and director of the Whole Brain Corp. finds kaleidoscopes a wonderful tool in determining right or left brain dominance. The mission of the Whole Brain Corp. of which Herrmann is founding president, is to apply new understandings of the brain to the human development needs of individuals and corporations throughout the world.

"To us, the turning of a kaleidoscope symbolizes the rearranging of stored information to constantly create new patterns — new approaches to problem solving — different colors change patterns of feelings."

Teaching people how to see things and change their patterns of thinking is part of the work accomplished at his Applied Creative Thinking Workshops. During more than 55 of these workshops, Herrmann determined that creativity "is a definable and teachable process that can be learned and applied."

Creativity experts emphasize the importance of expanding our horizons, and developing a healthy curiosity about things beyond our immediate field.

Since dominance is acquired more by nurture than by nature, it is quite possible to change a person's brain dominance profile through education, skill training and life experiences. If a left-brained person wants to stimulate the right side, he might develop an interest in kaleidoscopes.

The following description of the right brain explains why "kaleidopeople" have a right-hemisphere dominance.

> "The right brain is our visual brain. It is where we recognize faces as contrasted to names, and it is where we do our non-verbal thinking. For most of us, it is the center of intuitive and insightful thinking where we can process information simultaneously and where conceptual thinking can take place. It is the location of our ability to synthesize as opposed to analyze and this is where we can deal with holistic concepts, that is, where we can see the forest as opposed to the trees. Other parts of the right hemisphere are specialized in the areas of interpersonal processing, emotional thinking, and music appreciation."

This is the day-dreamer's corner, the area that allows the thinker to "see the big picture" — read signs of coming change, invent innovative solutions to problems and recognize new possibilities. Right brainers view from a whole point of view, seeing the end at the beginning and they need a lot of space.

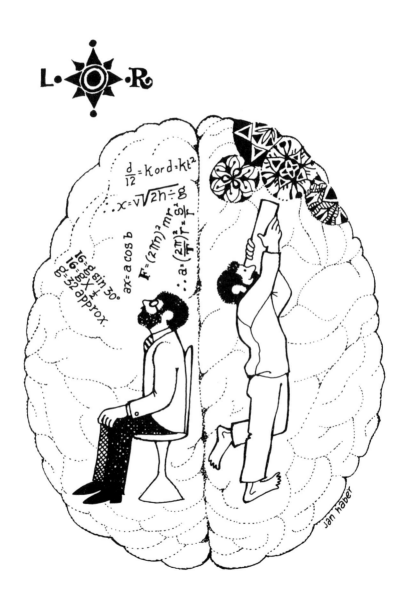

Collectable and Salable

While the non-verbal communication of kaleidoscopes transcends words, just introduce two collectors and the communication becomes quite vocal. Sharing and swapping scoops on scopes is almost as exhilarating for a scope-lover as unearthing an old Bush or discovering a good source for new kaleidoscopes.

One collector in New York says, "I head for them whenever I feel depressed — and it isn't only looking into them, it's just knowing they are there like friends. When I was a child, books were my friends. They were sold and I miss them. Now, kaleidoscopes help recapture my childhood."

Jim Lovell, another collector, says "kaleidoscopes are like Baroque music — something you can enjoy and revel in by yourself."

One couple in Alexandria, Virginia use their scopes as an intercom; leaving messages for one another in the form of an especially beautiful image to be shared.

Irene Walker believes that looking into a scope before going to sleep will put color into dreams. She keeps an assortment of scopes in her guest room so her guests can discover the joy of kaleidoscopes and dream in technicolor.

In California, Pat Seaman expresses it this way. "There is something magical about kaleidoscopes. I don't understand it, I just accept it. Everytime I get a new scope, no matter what the price, it is my 'favorite child' for awhile, then it joins the rest of the family."

Eric Sinizer, owner of the Light Opera Gallery in San Francisco's Ghiradelli Square, did for the marketing of kaleidoscopes what the article in the Smithsonian Magazines accomplished in the way of interest and enthusiasm. He was the first to carry an inventory truly representative of the emerging new images.

Eric's involvement with kaleidoscopes is a direct outgrowth of his primary interest in glass. He purchased his first scope at a crafts fair and enjoyed watching the transmission of light through it so much that he got another one — and then another. He uses his treasure trove of a gallery for his personal museum, so he put the scopes in his shop so he could enjoy them.

To his surprise, Eric discovered there are a great number who appreciate and collect kaleidoscopes. He began amassing the largest collection of scopes available anywhere, just as he had done with Russian lacquer boxes and fine glass. He was then the first to publish a catalog devoted solely to kaleidoscopes. Its colorful pictures and succinct descriptions have made it a hit everywhere. Now many shops and galleries across the country are featuring kaleidoscopes as an important part of their displays. (Appendix I contains a list of galleries and shops that feature at least six scope-makers.)

Julian Baird, president of Tree's Place in Orleans, Massachusetts, says it was Eric Sinizer's encouragement and unselfishly shared information about kaleidoscope designers that made his life richer and "in far more significant ways than monetary terms."

Julian has been interested in mandalic images for a long time. To him, kaleidoscopic patterns "embody both the static and the dynamic, both earthly and eternal, both still-point and turning wheel of time and space."

The rural coastal resort area of Cape Cod may seem an unlikely place to find what is probably the most extensive selection of kaleidoscopes at retail in the country; but then, Tree's Place is not the usual store. In addition to extensive groupings of other imported and domestic fine arts and crafts, Tree's Place features the work of about forty different artisans of kaleidoscopes in prices ranging from under $10 to over $1000.

Perhaps the best news for those who do not live near a dealer specializing in kaleidoscopes is that Tree's Place has just produced a video tape catalog of these instruments, available in both VHS and Beta home formats. Baird explains that this medium is perfectly suited to kaleidoscopes, since it allows the viewer to experience the colors and changing images produced by these instruments in a way that still photography can only suggest.

Hand of the Craftsman in Nyack, New York is another kaleidoscope mecca. Over two dozen artists are represented in the scope department of this craft gallery. The Habers' early involvement with kaleidoscopes is a delightful story.

Shel and Jan met as young undergraduates in art school. Romance blossomed and upon deciding to "go steady" they exchanged gifts. Shel gave Jan an optical prism that scattered rainbows everywhere and she gave him a kaleidoscope. Thirty years later, they are still exchanging optical toys and delighting each other with kaleidoscopes.

Sharing their scopes and encouraging visitors to play have become a way of life at Hand of the Craftsman. Jan explains, "Kaleidoscopes are practically a definition of our gallery's philosophy: that the creative arts, which feed the soul, are also great fun. We have always made special effort to obtain playful objects for our shop, things that are beautifully crafted and a joy to the hand and eye as well as amusing to experience."

In the early days of their shop, before they could find good hand-crafted scopes, Jan got simple toy models and dressed them up in fancy macrame, old lace and fold-dyed rice paper. It's quite a different story today as new kaleidoscopes become more and more decorative.

In addition to managing their busy, fun shop, the Habers are also involved with graphic arts and film animations. No telling what wondrous things are on the way either, because some exciting scope-related projects are in the planning stage. Meanwhile Nyack's Street Fairs, held each May and October, provide a perfect setting for a kaleidoscopic festival — outdoor jumbo scopes, glassblowers, kites, surprises — and who knows, maybe a magic carpet!

Hanson Galleries in Houston, Texas is recognized as one of the outstanding leaders in promoting American fine crafts. In their two handsome galleries, Art and Donna Milstein represent this growing movement with the very best in ceramics, wood, hand-blown glass and a by-product of mixed media — you guessed it, kaleidoscopes.

An early fascination with color, change and patterns, was evidenced in Donna's high school yearbook. As editor of the 1962 Po Hi (Ponca City Senior High School in Oklahoma) yearbook, Donna chose Kaleidoscope for the theme. The topic, the ideas and bits and pieces of her editorial comments all seem to tumble about in a prophecy of the very things that were to be a part of Donna's active, artistic, productive and kaleidoscopic career.

" . . . activities . . . a spirit . . . the people . . . reflecting . . . different and new ways of thinking . . . always a changing interpretation . . . a new approach . . . . We came to Po-Hi, new to it all, and pushed our ideas and our ways and ourselves into the pattern. We turned it and moved it, sometimes with joy and cheers, or grief or worry. It twisted at our touch and a pattern emerged, and it was the same after all, but different than the years before. It was hard to hold onto, or show someone else, as it changed all the time . . . even as we touched it and held it in our hands, it changed . . . ."

Mediscope

For some, the kaleidoscope is a "happening" — a joyous experience — a celebration of color. For others, it is a meditative device, a lens opening onto inspirational strata of rarified light.

Even Webster, with his vast comprehension, did not fully fathom the myriad facets of the kaleidoscope. So, I have coined a new word — Mediscope: to meditate as you look through a kaleidoscope, and breathe the colors, while listening to music.

Meditation is a natural process and we discover it at some stage of the soul's development. It is for the purpose of realizing, attuning and centering with the Supreme Life Force. Color meditation is not new, but the mode of procedure has always entailed mentally recalling a color and then concentrating on it. How much easier and more efficient to visually observe the color, and more than one color, an endless mixture of shades in splendorous patterns — to breathe and absorb the essence of color, to feel and assimilate color's energy. It is a calming yet exhilerating experience to look through a kaleidoscope at a spectrum of various hues until you find tones that influence your moods, elevate your emotions and feed your feelings — the color that is right for you.

In order to mediscope, it is important to open the windows of your inner space: to welcome in the light and let a gentle breeze stir ideas and feelings around until thoughts and attitudes are lifted up, until you feel enveloped in an aura from the rainbow of the musical spectrum, until there is an intuitive knowing that all the pieces are falling into place, and you feel at peace.

"Get yourselves a new heart
and a new spirit!
. . . Turn, and live." — *Ezek. 18:31, 32*

As a child I used to wish upon the first evening star. Now each morning I look into a kaleidoscope and as the first multi-faceted kaleidostar unfolds, I make a wish.

Today I make a special wish for each reader:
May your days be filled with vivacious patterns,
your dreams be steeped in color, and
the wish of your heart be granted!

Jan Haber

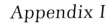

Appendix I

Shops and Galleries Featuring Kaleidoscopes

Abacus
8 McKown Street
Booth Bay Harbor, Maine 04538
(207) 633-2166

Albright-Knox Art Gallery
1285 Elmwood Avenue
Buffalo, New York 14222
(716) 882-8701

Appalachian Spring
1415 Wisconsin Avenue, N.W.
Washington, D.C. 20007
(202) 337-5780

The Artful Hand
Main Street Square
Orleans, Massachusetts 02653
(617) 255-2969

Artisans Gallery
Peddler's Village
Lahaska, Pennsylvania 18931
(215) 794-3112

Basic Blue
P.O. Box 59
Sugar Loaf, New York 10981
(914) 469-9208

Boulder Holding Co.
1107 Pearl Street
Boulder, Colorado 80302
(303) 443-4430

Craft Company No. 6
785 University Avenue
Rochester, New York 14607
(716) 473-3413

The Crafty Fox
80 Main Street
Nyack, New York 10960
(914) 358-5755

Dandelion
1700 Locust Street
Philadelphia, Pa. 19103
(215) 546-7655

Des Moines Art Center
Greenwood Park
Des Moines, Iowa 50312
(515) 277-4405

Design Center, Inc.
Bazaar del Mundo, Old Town
2754 Calhoun Street
San Diego, California 92110
(619) 298-1141

The Difference
23 E. College Avenue
Westerville, Ohio 43081
(614) 890-4151

Don Drumm Studios & Gallery
437 Crouse Street
Akron, Ohio 44311
(216) 253-6268

The Elements
14 Liberty Way
Greenwich, Connecticut 06830
(203) 661-0014

Fine Crafts Gallery
78 Woodlake Square
Houston, Texas 77063
(713) 789-8170

From Gifted Hands
Tlaquepaque Arts & Crafts
Sedona, Arizona 86336
(602) 282-4822

The Gadfly
215 S. Union Street
Alexandria, Virginia 22314
(703) 548-0218

The Gift Center
California Museum of Science,
    Industry and Aerospace
    Complex
700 State Dr. — Exposition Park
Los Angeles, California 90037
(213) 749-0366

Great Things
#769 Beverly Center
8522 Beverly Boulevard
Los Angeles, California 90048
(213) 659-0592

Hand of the Craftsman
58 S. Broadway
Nyack, New York 10960
(914) 358-6622

Handcrafters Gallery
44 Exchange Street
Portland, Maine 04101
(207) 772-4880

Hanson Galleries
Galleria II — Level 3
Houston, Texas 77056
(713) 552-1242

Hanson Galleries
Town and Country Center
Level 1, Suite G 137
Houston, Texas 77024
(713) 984-1242

High Tide, Rock Bottom
1814 Coventry Raod
Cleveland Heights, Ohio 44118
(216) 321-8500

Kaleidoscope
Dartsmouth Savings Bank
    Building
Hanover, New Hampshire 03755
(603) 643-4327

Kaleidoscope Gift Shop
146 Main Street
Northport, New York 11768
(516) 754-1134

Kentucky Center for the Arts
Gift Shop
5 Riverfront Plaza
Louisville, Kentucky 40202
(502) 562-0165

Light Opera Gallery
Ghirardelli Square #102
San Francisco, California 94109
(415) 775-7665

Midland Crafters
N.C. Route 2 Midland Road
Pinehurst, North Carolina 28374
(919) 295-6156

The Mole Hole
Phipps Plaza
3500 Peachtree Road
Atlanta, Georgia 30326
(404) 231-4840

The Mole Hole
210 Peachtree Street
Atlanta, Georgia 30303
(404) 584-6184

The Mole Hole
234 S. Washington Square
Lansing, Michigan 48933
(517) 482-2333

The Mole Hole at the Crossing
8702 Keystone Crossing
Indianapolis, Indiana 46240
(317) 846-3291

Mole Hole of Jacksonville
9911 Bay Meadow Road
Grande Boulevard Mall
Jacksonville, Florida 32216
(904) 641-9425

J. S. Morgan's
Southwest Plaza
8501 W. Bowles Avenue
Littleton, Colorado 80123
(303) 979-3058

New Morning Gallery
7 Boston Way
Asheville, North Carolina 28803
(704) 274-2831

The Old Moon
3016 Lower Greenville Avenue
Dallas, Texas 75206
(214) 827-9921

Past, Present & Future
24 S. 18th Street
Philadelphia, Pennsylvania
    19103
(215) 854-0444

Performer's Outlet
222 E. 85th Street
New York, New York 10128
(212) 249-8435

Pickering Galleries
Brentwood Place
Brentwood, Tennessee 37027
(615) 377-4667

The Quest of Sausalito
795 Bridgeway
Sausalito, California 94965
(415) 332-6832

The Red Balloon
1073 Wisconsin Avenue, N.W.
Washington, D.C. 20007
(202) 965-1200

Salamandra Glass, Ltd.
133-143 Market Street
Portsmouth, New Hampshire
    03801
(603) 341-4511

Scherer Gallery
93 School Road, West
Marlboro, New Jersey 07746
(201) 536-9471

Signature Gallery
Dock Square
North Street
Boston, Massachusetts 02109
(617) 227-4885

Star Magic
743 Broadway
New York, New York 10003
(212) 228-7770

Star Magic
4026A 24th Street
San Francisco, California 94114
(215) 641-8626

Tomlinson Craft Collection
519 N. Charles Street
Baltimore, Maryland 21201
(301) 539-6585

Tree's Place
6A at 28
Orleans, Massachusetts 02653
(617) 255-1330

Unicorn
15 Central Street
Woodstock, Vermont 05091
(802) 457-2480

Watersweeper & the Dwarf
717 Grand Avenue
Glenwood Springs, Colorado
    81601
(303) 945-2000

Whippoorwill Crafts
126 S. Market Building
Faneuil Hall Marketplace
Boston, Massachusetts 02109
(617) 523-5179

Windseye
3647 W. Hillsborough Avenue
Tampa, Florida 33614
(813) 875-9956

Appendix II

Brewster Patent

A.D. 1817 .... N° 4136.

Kaleidoscopes.

BREWSTER'S SPECIFICATION.

TO ALL TO WHOM THESE PRESENTS SHALL COME, I, David Brewster, of Edinburgh, Doctor of Laws, send greeting.

WHEREAS His present most Excellent Majesty King George the Third did by His Royal Letters Patent under the Great Seal of the United Kingdom of Great Britain and Ireland, bearing date at Westminster, the Tenth day of July, in the fifty-seventh year of His reign, give and grant unto me, the said David Brewster, my executors, administrators, and assigns, His especial full power, sole privilege and authority, that I, the said David Brewster, my executors, administrators, and assigns, during the term of years therein expressed, should and lawfully might make, use, exercise, and vend my NEW OPTICAL INSTRUMENT CALLED THE KALEIDOSCOPE FOR EXHIBITING AND TREATING BEAUTIFUL FORMS AND PATTERNS, OF GREAT USE IN ALL THE ORNAMENTAL ARTS within England, Wales, and the Town of Berwick-upon-Tweed, in such manner as to me, the said David Brewster, my executors, administrators, and designs should in our discretion seem meet; in which said Letters Patent is certified a proviso that if I, the said David Brewster, should not particularly describe and ascertain the nature of my said Invention, and in what manner the same is to be performed, by an instrument in writing under my hand and seal, and cause the same to be inrolled in His Majesty's High Court of Chancery within two calendar months next and immediately after the date of the said Letters Patent, that then the said Letters Patent, and all liberties and advantages whatsoever thereby granted, should utterly cease, determine, and become void, as in and by the said recited Letters Patent, relation being there unto had, may more fully and at large appear.

NOW KNOW YE, that in compliance with the said proviso, I, the said David Brewster, do hereby declare that the nature of my said Invention, and in what manner the same is to be performed, are particularly described and ascertained in manner following (that is to say):—

The kaleidoscope (from καλος beautiful; ειδος, a form; and σκοπεω to see) is an instrument for creating and exhibiting an infinite variety of beautiful forms, and is constructed in such a manner as either to please the eye by an ever-varying succession of splendid tints and symmetrical forms, or to enable the observer to render permanent such as may appear most appropriate for any of the numerous branches of the ornamental arts. This instrument in its most common form consists of two reflecting surfaces inclined to each other at any angle, but more properly at an angle which is an aliquot part of 360°. The reflecting surfaces may be two plates of glass plain or quicksilvered, or two metallic surfaces, or the two inner surfaces of a solid prism of glass or rock chrystal, from which the light suffers total reflection. The plates should vary in length according to the focal distance of the eye; 5, 6, 7, 8, 9, and 10 inches will in general be most convenient; or they may be made only 1, 2, 3, or 4 inches long, provided distinct vision is obtained at one end by placing at the other end an eye glass whose focal length is equal to the length of the reflecting planes. The inclination of the reflectors that is in general most pleasing is 18°, 20°, or 22½°, or the 20th, 18th, and 16th part of a circle; but the planes may be set at any required angle either by a metallic, a paper, or cloth joint, or any other simple contrivance. When the two planes are put together with their straightest and smoothest edges in contact, they will have the form shewn in Figure 1, where A, B, C, is the aperture or angle formed by the plates. In this Figure the

FIG. I.

plates are rectangular, but it may often be more convenient to give them the triangular form shewn at M, Fig. 2, or N, Fig. 3.

134

When the instrument
is thus constructed,
it may be either cov-
ered up with paper
or leather or placed
in a cylindrical or
any other tube, so

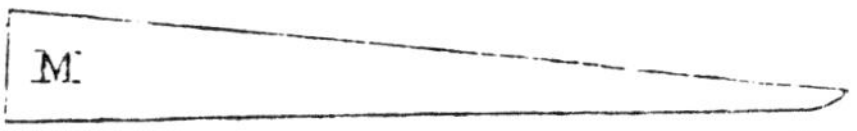

FIG.2.

FIG.3.

that the aperture A, B, C may be left completely open, and also
a small aperture at the angular point D. If the eye is now
placed at D, and looks thro' the aperture A, B, C, it will perceive
a brilliant circle of light, divided into as many sectors as the
number of times that the angle of the reflector is contained in
360°. If this angle is 18° the number of sectors will be 20°; and
whatever be the form of the aperture A, B, C, the luminous
space seen thro' the instrument will be a figure produced by
the arrangement of 20 of these apertures round C as a centre,
in consequence of the successive reflexions between the polished surfaces. Hence, it follows, that if any object, however
ugly or irregular in itself, is placed before the aperture A, B, C,
the part of it that can be seen through the aperture will be seen
also in every sector, and every image of the object will coalesce
into a form mathematically symmetrical and highly pleasing
to the eye. If the object is put in motion, the combination of
images will likewise be put in motion, and new forms, perfectly
different but equally symmetrical, will successively present
themselves, sometimes vanishing in the centre, sometimes
emerging from it, and sometimes playing around in double and
opposite oscillations. When the object is tinged with different
colours, the most beautiful tints are developed in succession,
and the whole figure delights the eye by the perfection of its
forms and the brilliancy of its colouring. The motion of the
object may be effected either by the hand or by a simple piece
of mechanism, or the same effect may be produced by the motion of the instrument over the object or round its own axis. In
the form of the kaleidoscope now described the object should
be held close to the aperture A, B, C, and the eye should be
placed as nearly as possible in the line C, D, for the figure loses
its symmetry in proportion as the object recedes from A, B, C,
and as the eye rises above D. The instrument is therefore
limited in its present form to the use of objects which can be
held close to the aperture. In order to remove the limitation,
the tube which contains the reflectors should slide in another

tube of nearly the same length, and having a convex lens at its further extremity; the focal length of the lens should be always less than its greatest distance from the aperture A, B, C. In general it should be about ⅓ or ¼ of that distance, but it will be adviseable to have two or even three lenses of different focal lengths to fit into the end of the outer tube, and to be used as circumstances may require, or a variation of focal length may be produced by the separation or approach of two lenses. When the instrument is thus fitted up it may be applied to objects at all distances, and these objects, whose images are formed in an inverted position at the aperture A, B, C, may be introduced into the symmetrical picture in the very same manner as if they were brought close to the instrument. Hence, we can introduce trees, flowers, statues, and living animals, and any object which is too large to be comprehended by the aperture A, B, C, may be removed to such a distance that its image is sufficiently reduced. The kaleidoscope is also constructed with three or more reflecting planes, which may be arranged in various ways. The tints placed before the aperture may be the complementary colors produced by transmitting polarised light thro' regularly chrystallized bodies or pieces of glass that have received the polarising structure. The partial polarisation of the light by successive reflexions occasions a partial analysis of the transmitted light; but in order to develope the tints with brilliancy, the analysis of the light must procede its admission into the aperture. Instead of looking thro' the extremity D of the tube, the effects which have been described may be exhibited to many persons at once, upon the principle of the solar microscope or magic lanthorn, and in this way, or by the application of the camera lucida, the figures may be accurately delineated. It would be an endless task to point out the various purposes in the ornamental arts to which the kaleidoscope is applicable. It may be sufficient to state, that it will be of great use for architects, ornamental painters, plasterers, jewellers, carvers and gliders, cabinet makers, wire workers, bookbinders, calico printers, carpet manufacturers, manufacturers of pottery, tery, and every other profession in which ornamental patterns are required. The painter may introduce the very colours which he is to use; the jeweler, the jewels which he is to arrange; and in general, the artist may apply to the instrument the materials which he is to embody, and thus form the most correct opinion of their effect when combined into an ornamental pattern.

When the instrument is thus applied, an infinity of patterns are created , and the artist can select such as he considers most suitable to his work. When a knowledge of the nature and powers of the instrument has been acquired by a little practice, he will be able to give any character to the pattern that he chooses, and he may even create a series of different patterns, all rising out of one another and returning by similar gradations to the first pattern of the series. In all these cases the pattern is perfectly symmetrical round a centre, or all the images of the aperture A, B, C, are exactly alike; but this symmetry may be altered, for after the pattern is drawn it may be reduced into a square, a triangular, an elliptical, or any other form that we please. The instrument will give annular patterns by keeping the reflectors separate as at A, B, Fig. 4, and it will give rectilineal ones by placing the reflectors parallel to each other, as in Fig. 5. The kaleidoscope is also proposed as an instrument of amusement to please the eye by the creation and exhibition of beautiful forms in the same manner as the ear is delighted by the combination of musical sounds. When Custillon proposed the construction of an ocular harpsichord, he was mistaken in supposing that any combination of harmonic colors could afford the pleasure to the person who viewed them, for it is only when these colors are connected with regular and beautiful forms that the eye is gratified by the combination. The kaleidoscope, therefore, seems to realise the idea of an ocular harpsichord.

In witness whereof, I, the said David Brewster, have hereunto set my hand and seal, this Twenty-seventh day of August, in the year of our Lord One thousand eight hundred and seventeen.

DAVID (L.S.) BREWSTER

Signed and sealed by the within-named
David Brewster (being first duly
stamped) in the presence of us,
ARCH^D MONTGOMERY,
Witness, residing at Wherin,
Parish of Newlands, and County of Peebles.
ROB^T MONTGOMERY,
Of Lincoln's Inn,
Barrister at Law.

UNITED STATES PATENT OFFICE

CHARLES G. BUSH, OF BOSTON, MASSACHUSETTS, ASSIGNOR
TO HIMSELF AND JOHN W. HOARD.

IMPROVEMENT IN KALEIDOSCOPES.

Specification forming part of Letters Patent No. 143,271, dated September 30,
1873; reissue No. 5,649, dated November 11, 1873; application filed
October 30, 1873.

To all whom it may concern:

Be it known that I, CHARLES G. BUSH, of Boston, in the county of Suffolk
and State of Massachusetts, have invented a new and useful Improved Object
for the Object-Box of Kaleidoscopes; . . .

In the rotation of the object-box, my compound tube, like any other object
therein, is caused by gravity to fall into different positions.

A hollow glass object with two immiscible liquids and an air-bubble, contained therein is shown in Figs. 2 and 3, in which b is the vessel hermetically
sealed, c and c^1 the two immiscible liquids, and d the air-bubble, the whole
resembling a diminutive glass spirit-level.

I would remark that a glass tube, containing a single liquid and an air-
bubble, the ends of the tube being closed by cement or plugging, is an object
heretofore used by me, and not claimed in this application; and in carrying
out my invention, in regard to the contents of the tube, I employ either two or
more liquids of different den-
sities or character, or a liquid
with or a liquid with a solid or
solids. I thus obtain two liquids
or objects of different colors
within the same vessel or tube,
and which, by their relative
movements within such tube,
produce new and pleasing effects.

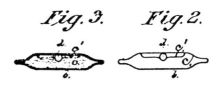

What I claim, therefore, as new in objects for the object-box of kaleidoscopes,
is as follows:

1. In combination with a kaleidoscope-box, a glass tube or vessel for containing one or more objects, said tube or vessel being closed hermetically without
the use or cement or plugging.

2. In combination with a kaleidoscope-box, an object, consisting of a glass
tube or vessel containing liquid, and closed hermetically by the fusing of the
glass without the aid of cement or plugging.

3. An object for kaleidoscopes, consisting of a glass tube or vessel containing
two or more immiscible liquids, or one or more liquids and one or more solids.

CHARLES G. BUSH.

IMPROVEMENT IN OBJECT-BOXES FOR KALEIDOSCOPES.

Specification forming part of Letters Patent No. 151,006, dated May 19, 1874;
application filed March 20, 1874.

Be it known that I, CHAS. G. BUSH, of Boston, Massachusetts, have invented
an Improvement in Object-Boxes for Kaleidoscopes, of which the following is
a specification:

My invention consists in making the object-box of a kaleidoscope with an
opening, and a cover for the same, for the ready introduction into or removal
of the objects from the box, thus avoiding the necessity, as the boxes have been
heretofore constructed, of taking the whole apparatus apart, and removing one
of the glasses of the box, and then putting the parts together again.

I claim —

A kaleidoscope object-box, provided with an opening and movable cover therefor, substantially as and for the purpose set forth.

CHARLES G. BUSH.

IMPROVEMENT IN KALEIDOSCOPES.

Specification forming part of Letters Patent No. 151,005, dated May 19, 1874; application filed December 20, 1873.

To all whom it may concern:

Be it known that I, CHAS. G. BUSH, of Boston, Massachusetts, have invented Improvements in Kaleidoscope, of which the following is a specification:

My present invention consists in combining, with a rotating object-box, a means between the eye and object-box, for illuminating the objects, so that opaque objects, equally as well as transparent ones, may be employed, and their colors fully displayed. It further consists in uniting in the same instrument the requisites for displaying properly the true colors both of opaque and trans-lucent objects; in other words, merging, virtually, the two characters of instru-ments into one. It further consists in combining, with a kaleidoscope having a revolving object-box, a variegated colored card-board or reflector, to be hung behind the instrument upon a stationary support, so that a background of any desired tint or color may be brought at will behind the object-glass, and thus give such background for the figure or design presented to the eye.

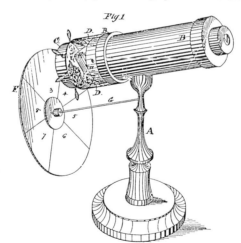

Fig 1

I claim —

1. The combination, in a kaleidoscope for opaque objects, of an independent revolving object-box, supported in near proximity to the objective end of the prism, and a transparent tube surrounding the objective end of the prism, and also serving as the support of said revolving box.

2. The combination, with a kaleidoscope for opaque objects, as described, of an independent revolving object-box, whose ends are both of glass, either perfectly plain, or the outer one ground and the inner one clear, for use either with the transparent or opaque objects.

3. In combination with a kaleidoscope, the parti-colored reflectng card-board, adjustable, by rotation, to afford a series of backgrounds of any desired color, substantially as shown and described.

CHARLES G. BUSH.

IMPROVEMENT IN KALEIDOSCOPE-STANDS.

Specification forming part of Letters Patent No. 156,875, dated November 17, 1874; application filed May 22, 1874.

To all whom it may concern:

Be it known that I, CHAS. G. BUSH, of Boston, State of Massachusetts, have invented an Improvement in Stands for Parlor-Kaleidoscopes, &c., of which the following is a specification:

My improvement relates to the mode of constructing the stand and its legs, used for supporting a parlor-kaleidoscope and for similar purposes, the object being to facilitate the packing them in a small compact compass for transportation or storing away, and yet to readily put the same together firmly for use without the use of glue, nails, rivets, or any fastening device.

Heretofore kaleidoscope-stands for parlor use have been made with the standard or post secured or screwed into a solid block or base, which needed to be of considerable diameter, and was of thick expensive wood.

I claim —

The stand constructed with the cross-cuts in the post, and with the central cross-cuts in the cross-pieces which compose the legs or base, the whole being fitted and adapted to be united and held together by pressure and frictional contact only, and to be instantly taken apart, in the manner and for the purpose shown and described.

CHARLES G. BUSH.

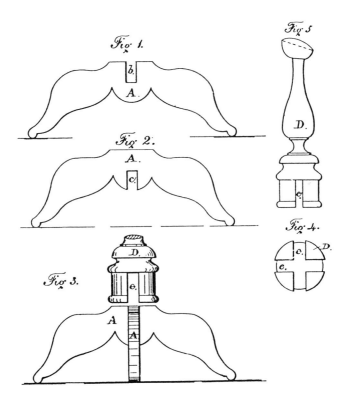

Brewster, Sir David, A Treatise on the Kaleidoscope (Edinburgh: Archibald Constable & Co., 1819)

Brewster, Sir David, The Kaleidoscope — Its History, Theory and Construction with its application to the fine and useful arts, second, enlarged edition (London: John Murray, 1858)

"Description of the Patent Kaleidoscope Invented by Dr. Brewster," Blackwood's Magazine, Edinburgh, May 1818, v.3 No. 14 pp. 121-123.

"History of Dr. Brewster's Kaleidoscope, with remarks on its supposed resemblance to other plain mirrors. Blackwood's Magazine, Edinburgh, June 1818, v.3 No. 15, pp. 331-337.

"The Homelife of Sir David Brewster," by his daughter Mrs. Gordon, The Southern Review, January 1874, v.14 No. 29, pp. 53-80.

Letter from James Hogg To James Frazer, Frazer's Magazine for Town and Country, v.6 Aug. Dec. 1832

"On the Kaleidoscope," by P. M. Roget, Annals of Philosophy, Jan.-June, 1818, v.11 article 15 pp. 375-378

Sir David Brewster, The Living Age, (from the Portrait Gallery), July 2, 1859, No. 788, third series No. 66, pp. 3-7.

Bibliography — Color

Arguelles, Jose and Miriam, Mandala (Shambhala, Colo. 1972)

Birren, Faber, Color Psychology and Color Therapy (New Jersey: Citadel Press 1950)

Clark, Linda, The Ancient Art of Color Therapy (New York: Pocket Books, 1975)

Don, Frank, Color Your World (New York: Destiny Books, 1983)

Graham, F. Lanier, ed., The Rainbow Book (New York: Vintage Books, Division of Random House 1979)

Heline, Corinne, Color and Music in the New Age California: DeVorss & Co., 1964)

Heline, Corinne, Healing and Regeneration Through Color (California: DeVorss & Co., 1980)

Jackson, Carole, Color Me Beautiful (Washington, D.C.: Acropolis Books, 1980)

Jones, Alex, Seven Mansions of Color (California: DeVorss & Co., 1982)

Jung, C. G., Mandala Symbolism (New Jersey: Princeton University Press, 1972)

Kargere, Audrey, Color and Personality (Maine: Samuel Weiser, 1949)

Index

Après la Pluie, 90, 102
Auger, Stephen, 41, 49, 100
Baird, Julian, 126
Bennett, Carolyn, 31, 49, 56, 98, 112
Bits of the Past, 46, 59
Brewster, Sir David, 13, 51, 133
Brickel, Alfred, 92
Bush, Charles G, 17, 49, 138
C. Bennett Scopes, see Bennett
Chesnik-Koch, Ltd., 45, 57
Chesshire, Howard, 21, 26, 61
Chromoscopes, 79
Classical Glass, 44, 59
Colley, Carmen and Stephen, 65, 99
Color, 114
Colorscopes by Holler, 109, 117
Colorscopes by Kosage, 85, 101
Comeau, Peg and Dennis, 44, 59
Culver, John, 72, 97
Ecuyer, Bill and Irene, 46, 59
Efrocine, 114
Endress, Marilyn, 82, 103
Fantasy Glass by Lesley, 59, 88
For Your Eyes, 83, 104
Galaxy Glassworks, 78, 104
Gallocolley Glass, 65, 99
Gemscope, 82, 103
Glossary, 21
Golden Mary, 110, 119
Goral, Helmut and Charlene, 122
Grannis, Tim, 84, 103
Greenberg, Annie, 78, 104
Haber, Jan and Shel, 126
Herrmann, Ned, 123
Holler, Irene, 109, 117
Howlett, Ray, 102, 111, 118
Huber, Craig, 78, 104
Johnson, Doug, 29, 55, 98
Kaleidoplex, 93, 98
Kaleidoscopia, 75, 107

Kaleidostitch, see Saber
Kaleidovisions, 34, 58, 98
Kalish, David, 79
Karadimos, Charles, 49, 76, 107
Karascope, see Karelitz
Karelitz, Judith, 23, 49, 54, 112
Kaufman, Kenneth, 110, 116
Kent, Dean, 41, 49, 100
Kerby, Joe, 83, 104
Koch, Sheryl, 45, 57
Kosage, Cheryl and Ken, 85, 101
Laughing Coyote, see Lee
Lazarowski, Jack, 84, 103
Lee, Claudia and Ron, 39, 105
Mandala, 113
Mandala Candles, see Goral
Mandala Kaleidoscopes, 26, 61
Marbelo-Scope, 69
Marshall, Dorothy, 25, 57
Mediscope, 128
Milstein, Art and Donna, 127
Morehead, Robert and Stella, 86, 105
MS Designs, 43
Musser, Craig, 36, 53, 143, covers
Newlin, Gary, 91
Northampton Studios, 41, 49, 100
O'Connor, Bill, 36, 53, 143, covers
Oz Optics, see Marshall
P-BAR-K Productions, 48, 63
Palosky, Rick, 64, 86
Paretti, Carol and Tom, 62, 81
Potter, Dee, 60, 68
Prism Design, 84, 103
Proctor, Tom, 61, 66, 98
Quilts, see Golden
Raccioppi, Rose, 40
Reike, Walter, 93, 98
Reynolds, Peach, 34, 58, 98
Roberts, Ann and Pete, 74
Roe, Howard, 91
Ross, Sue, 69

Saber, Mary Ann, 109, 121
Scepter Scopes, 72, 97
Seaman, Pat, 43, 125
Sinizer, Eric, 125
Souza, Carrie, 47, 59
Spirit Scopes, 89, 106
Stained Glass Kaleidoscopes,
    see Karadimos
Stasi, Jeff and Tina, 75, 107
Stephan, Robert, 111, 118
Stevenson, Willie and Alice, 89,
    106
Stora, Dominic, 90, 102
Stover, Susan, 43
Tompkins, Brian, 110, 120
Touch of Glass, 91

Van Cort, Erik and Kate, 49, 70,
    108
Van Cort Instruments, Ltd.,
    see Van Cort
Van Dyke, Ltd., 36, 53, 143, covers
Victorian Visions, 86, 105
Wadsworth, Lesley, 59, 88
Webber, Kirk, 48, 63
Weeks, Corki, 63, 67
Whole Brain Corp., 123
Windseye, 29, 59, 98
Wooden puzzle sculpture,
    see Tompkins
Workingwood, 62, 81
Yaeger, Marshall, 93, 98

Van Dyke, Series III

About the Author

Other books by Cozy Baker include "A Cozy Getaway," "Holiday Frame of Mind," and "Love Beyond Life." As a world traveler she has written numerous travel articles for newspapers and magazines.

Cozy is also known for her public speaking. Her topics explore intriguing places to sojourn, as well as inner journeys which lead to spiritual joy and peace.

Recently Cozy has turned her attention to the fascinating world of kaleidoscopes. After acquiring one of the premier collections of both old and new scopes, she undertook the organization and coordination of the first major exhibition of kaleidoscopes in America, at Strathmore Hall Arts Center in suburban Washington, D.C.

A long-time resident of this area, Cozy lives with her attorney husband Hal, son Brant, two cats and 10,000 flowers.

Between planning programs and staging fund raisers for charitable and civic organizations, Cozy is working on the establishment of a permanent kaleidoscope museum; hopefully one that can sponsor traveling exhibitions to all parts of the country, and even the world.